Feminist Theory After Deleuze

DELEUZE ENCOUNTERS

Series Editor: Ian Buchanan, Professor and Director of the Institute for Social Transformation Research, University of Wollongong, Australia.

The Deleuze Encounters series provides students in philosophy and related subjects with concise and accessible introductions to the application of Deleuze's work in key areas of study. Each book demonstrates how Deleuze's ideas and concepts can enhance present work in a particular field.

Series titles include:

Cinema After Deleuze, Richard Rushton
Philosophy After Deleuze, Joe Hughes
Political Theory After Deleuze, Nathan Widder
Theology After Deleuze, Kristien Justaert
Space After Deleuze, Arun Saldanha
Media After Deleuze, David Savat and Tauel Harper
Music After Deleuze, Edward Campbell

Feminist Theory After Deleuze

HANNAH STARK

Bloomsbury Academic
An imprint of Bloomsbury Publishing Plc

BLOOMSBURY
LONDON • OXFORD • NEW YORK • NEW DELHI • SYDNEY

Bloomsbury Academic
An imprint of Bloomsbury Publishing Plc

50 Bedford Square   1385 Broadway
London   New York
WC1B 3DP   NY 10018
UK   USA

www.bloomsbury.com

BLOOMSBURY and the Diana logo are trademarks of Bloomsbury Publishing Plc

First published 2017

© Hannah Stark, 2017

Hannah Stark has asserted her right under the Copyright, Designs and Patents Act, 1988, to be identified as Author of this work.

All rights reserved. No part of this publication may be reproduced or transmitted in any form or by any means, electronic or mechanical, including photocopying, recording, or any information storage or retrieval system, without prior permission in writing from the publishers.

No responsibility for loss caused to any individual or organization acting on or refraining from action as a result of the material in this publication can be accepted by Bloomsbury or the author.

British Library Cataloguing-in-Publication Data
A catalogue record for this book is available from the British Library.

ISBN: HB: 9781472526854
        PB: 9781472529220
        ePDF: 9781472528766
        ePub: 9781472533340

Library of Congress Cataloging-in-Publication Data
A catalog record for this book is available from the Library of Congress.

Series: Deleuze Encounters

Typeset by Fakenham Prepress Solutions, Fakenham, Norfolk NR21 8NN

For Anne

CONTENTS

Acknowledgements ix
List of abbreviations xi

   Introduction 1

1 Thought 7
   Enlightenment legacies 8
   Feminism and liberal humanism 12
   Liberating thought 17

2 Becoming 25
   Becoming-woman 26
   The girl 34
   Feminism and the future 37

3 Desire 41
   Desire, psychoanalysis and experimental psychiatry 42
   The desiring-machines 49
   Eroticism 54

4 Bodies 61
   Sex and gender 63
   Sexual difference 66
   What can bodies do? 70

5   Difference 79
    Pure difference 80
    Identity and political representation 86
    Intersectional difference 93

6   Politics 99
    Recognition and politics 101
    Feminism beyond recognition 106
    A feminism of imperceptibility 111

Notes 117
Bibliography 123
Index 131

ACKNOWLEDGEMENTS

I would like to thank Ian Buchanan who suggested that I write this book and for other good advice along the way. Thanks to those at Bloomsbury involved in the editing and production process and to Madeleine Davis for compiling the index. I am very grateful to Luke Hortle for his meticulous eleventh-hour research assistance.

I would like to acknowledge those people who supported the germination of my interest in Deleuze when I was undertaking my PhD: Mandy Treagus who took on a risky project and gave me the time and space to work through ideas, Ken Ruthven who taught me that it was important to find clarity particularly when working on Deleuze and Jessica Murrell who worked beside me. I would also like to thank my family Jeff, Jordan and Ben Stark and Joyce Dinan, who (refreshingly) have very little interest in Deleuze but who support and encourage me in this work anyway.

Much gratitude goes to my colleagues at the University of Tasmania, particularly to Ralph Crane and the Elle Leane who were there when I ran into difficulties. Special thanks to Michelle Phillipov who not only kept me on track but who also told me when the book wasn't working, even when it was the last thing that I wanted to hear. I am appreciative to various collaborators who have pushed me to think about Deleuze and/or feminist theory in new ways: Tim Laurie, Jon Roffe and Guinevere Narraway. Many thanks to my students, particularly in my Literary Theory course and postgraduate theory reading group, who remind me of the wonder of encountering theory.

This book was written largely on weekends. I would like to thank Anne Romeo for her love and patience and for holding our life together while I worked.

LIST OF ABBREVIATIONS

A-O	*Anti-Oedipus*
ATP	*A Thousand Plateaus*
B	*Bergsonism*
BCD	'Bergson's Conception of Difference'
D	*Dialogues*
DI	*Desert Islands and Other Texts*
DR	*Difference and Repetition*
EP	*Expressionism in Philosophy: Spinoza*
K	*Kafka: Toward a Minor Literature*
LS	*The Logic of Sense*
NP	*Nietzsche and Philosophy*
PS	*Proust and Signs*
S	*Spinoza: Practical Philosophy*
TRM	*Two Regimes of Madness*
WIP?	*What is Philosophy?*

INTRODUCTION

Sometimes when we encounter new ideas they shock us out of the complacencies that inhere in accustomed ways of thinking. This was how I felt the first time that I encountered the work of Gilles Deleuze. In his review of *Difference and Repetition* and *The Logic of Sense*, Michel Foucault captures this capacity in Deleuze's work. He writes: 'a lightning storm was produced which will bear the name of Deleuze: new thought is possible; thought again is possible' (1977: 196). This book is interested in how Deleuze's work might shock feminist theory into finding novel ways to think about sexual difference and what it means socially, philosophically, politically and materially. It argues that Deleuze's work is useful for feminist theory not because he worked in a sustained way on women or gender, but instead because his work undermines the philosophical systems that have oppressed women since the Enlightenment. Deleuze's work is important for interrogating those systems of meaning that compose our philosophies. However it is also useful in the task of speculatively re-imagining, and materially re-creating, the possibilities for thinking and for living. In particular, this book is interested in how Deleuze's work makes new thought possible within feminist theory and looks for the vitality that it might bring to feminist debates. Simultaneously, it probes the way that feminist theory has changed the way that we read Deleuze by inviting us to ask alternative kinds of questions about his work.

One of the ways that Deleuze challenges complacent ways of thinking is through a method that could be described as creative destruction. He is not happy with simply renovating old and insufficient concepts. Instead, he annihilates our tired ideas in order to make way for the new. For Deleuze and his collaborator Félix Guattari, philosophy is 'the art of forming, inventing, and fabricating concepts' (WIP?: 2). Concepts offer us new ways to address the world. This is because the world throws up problems and is problematic. Here, problems are generative: they prompt us to new thoughts, new actions and new modes of being. If we look at feminist theory as a problem, we can see that it pushes us not just to critique the old, patriarchal regimes of thought but also that it requires us to find new concepts. Here, feminist theory provides us with a particular orientation in relation to the world, a framework for addressing patriarchy and the inequalities that it creates.

Turning to a male philosopher, and one who did not have much to say explicitly about feminism might seem, at first, like a manoeuvre that runs counter to the ideals of feminism. Feminist theory critiques the phallocentric nature of Western philosophy and the disproportionate amount of space that has historically been afforded to men's ideas. With this in mind we could question what it means to turn to a male philosopher to articulate a feminist position. However, if feminist theory ignores male philosophers and the dominance of male voices in the history of thought, it risks complicity with the erasure of a history of male privilege. The reality is that patriarchy has constrained women's capacity to contribute to philosophical debates for far too long. To counter this, feminists should co-opt any intellectual resource in the service of challenging the systems which have marginalized them. Furthermore, women should not be the only ones to whom the job of thinking politically about gender and power should fall. Feminism is neither women's job nor their responsibility. And, importantly, it is not their role to educate men about their oppression within patriarchy. As Audre Lorde insists, it is not the prerogative of those who are oppressed to educate their oppressors. Rather, those who are oppressed by patriarchy, by white privilege and by heteronormativity should use their energy 'in redefining [them]selves and devising realistic scenarios for altering the present and constructing the future' (2007: 115). However, this cannot end with the material and 'realistic' conditions of women under patriarchy. Feminist theory also needs to find a speculative register in which to imagine new ways to think, to create and to live.

This book provides a necessarily selective engagement with Deleuze's enormous body of work. It is structured by a series of concepts, which are both important to Deleuze's work and key concerns of feminist theory. It begins from the premise that thinking is at the foundation of philosophy. However, thought is not a neutral activity but has traditionally been gendered as masculine at the exclusion of women. Chapter 1 interrogates the philosophical systems, inherited from the Enlightenment, which have contributed to this problematic gendering of thought. Foremost amongst these systems is Cartesianism, which elevates the mind and associates it with masculinity while simultaneously devaluing the feminine and the body. This hierarchy contributes to a gendering of reason and rationality as masculine. Because rationality is an attribute that has designated the human, the exclusion of women from thought also marginalizes them in relation to this category. These discourses are embodied in the figure of Enlightenment man; held in place by liberal humanism, this is a normative and exclusionary model for the human. The chapter considers the emergence of feminist theory as a critique of the single (masculine) model of the human. In this way it provides an introduction to the major strands of feminist theory and asks what it means for women to think and contribute to knowledge. Deleuze poses a profound challenge to the gendering of thought through his critique of Cartesianism and re-valuing of the body. However, this chapter advances Deleuze's concept of thought itself as having significant potential for feminist theory. Not only does this concept repudiate the masculine purchase on reason but it also dislocates thought from the subject and extends it beyond the human. The new image of thought that Deleuze elaborates is the first act of creative destruction that we will consider, and it is exemplary of the way that Deleuze pushes us to find new and better concepts to address the world.

Chapter 2 turns to Deleuze and Guattari's concept of becoming, which they pose as an alternative to static states of being. Because all becomings are becoming-minor they enact a movement away from the universalizing figure of the subject as it is imagined in liberal humanism. Becoming is enacted first through becoming-woman before moving through a range of other becomings on the way to becoming-imperceptible. As the gateway to all other becomings, becoming-woman is a significant concept for feminist theory. However, it is also the concept that has been the focal point of the volatile encounter between feminists and Deleuze's work. The chapter examines this early feminist critique of Deleuze as exemplified by Luce Irigaray, Alice Jardine and Rosi Braidotti. It then turns to some of the more productive aspects of the concept of becoming for undermining the hierarchies that create forms of oppression such as patriarchy. For Deleuze and Guattari, the figure that exemplifies becoming-woman is the girl. This is not a concept that has received the same level of feminist attention as becoming-woman. As such this chapter examines the place of the girl throughout Deleuze's work as a figure that embodies the potentialities of becoming-minor. Becoming is always oriented to the future. This provides feminist theory with a useful mechanism for challenging essentialism, which constrains women's capacities through positing that characteristics culturally associated with femininity are actually innate. If feminist theory were to take seriously the futural nature of Deleuze's work, it would become better equipped to challenge so-called 'post-feminism'. As such, the chapter examines Deleuze's work as an antidote to post-feminism's concerning tendencies to posit feminism as a movement directed toward the attainment of discrete goals, which, once achieved, might relegate feminist theory to the past.

Chapter 3 examines Deleuze and Guattari's rejection of the psychoanalytic framing of desire as something that arises from the interiority of the subject and is directed at what the subject lacks. This is of great significance to feminist theory because within psychoanalysis, lack is always mapped onto women and, more specifically, onto their bodies. The chapter turns to *Anti-Oedipus*, examining its historical emergence and considering the reformulation of desire that Deleuze and Guattari offer. Instead of positioning desire as lack, they theorize it as a pre-personal force that is everywhere and productive of connections between things. Desire is anarchic, flowing along schizophrenic pathways and causing ruptures in organized systems. Desire is what animates the connections between things, which is why it is constitutive of desiring-machines. Consequently, desire, as Deleuze and Guattari describe it, could never have been contained in the Oedipal triangle or governed by the phallus. Although challenging the Oedipal configuration of desire entails rejecting the psychoanalytic model of the unconscious, and consequently freeing desire from sexuality and its associations with pleasure, this chapter argues that Deleuze's work enables new considerations of sexuality and intimate life beyond heteronormativity and reproduction and new possibilities for pleasure and eroticism.

Moving from the erotic body to the sexed specificity of bodies, Chapter 4 examines the ways that bodies are organized by sexual difference. It begins by establishing the classic feminist distinction between sex and gender, which is the predominant framework through which sexual difference has been understood in Anglo-American feminism. However, for Deleuze sexual difference is a product of a particular concept of subjectivity in a specific social milieu. Taking up Deleuze and Guattari's interrelated critique of capitalism and the Oedipal family structure, this chapter explains their analysis of the ways that bodies, which are infinitely different, are territorialized into the categories 'man' and 'woman'. The chapter then pivots to the active and affirmative body that Deleuze theorizes and which feminists have celebrated in relation to his work. It explains the significance of Deleuze's use of Spinoza's monism, in rejecting the philosophical and problematically gendered privileging of the mind over the body. As such Deleuze offers a way to argue against the denigration of the body (and of women) in Western philosophy, as outlined in Chapter 1. Deleuze's affirmative model of embodiment enables us to think about particular bodies not in terms of their conformity or otherwise to a normative ideal, but in terms of what they can do and become. These bodies are constantly engaged in forming temporary and contingent connections with other bodies – both human and nonhuman. This chapter examines the significant benefits of Deleuze's work about the body for thinking about bodies that do not conform to normative standards, such as disabled bodies. Because power oppresses a range of bodies that do not conform to the norm, this chapter argues that it is important for feminism to be attentive to embodied differences that go beyond sex.

Chapter 5 considers the concept of difference that Deleuze advances in *Difference and Repetition*, in which he argues for the existence of difference outside of the ways it is conventionally captured by identity, opposition, analogy and resemblance. For Deleuze, to conceive of difference solely in relation to these categories is to ignore a deeper form of untamed difference that is positive and generative. Within his ontology, being manifests itself through differential processes, which enable him to refuse the metaphysical primacy of identity and acknowledge the continual proliferation of difference. As such it is difference that is foundational; the effect of identity may emerge but this is always a secondary manifestation. The chapter explains the philosophical foundation of Deleuze's abstract rendering of difference before drawing out the implications of this framework for the ways that 'difference' and 'identity' are mobilized in feminist debates. The most important aspect of valuing difference over identity for feminist theory is that it challenges the salience of identity politics. This chapter examines the tension in Deleuze's work between molar categories such as 'woman' and the molecular and anti-identity politics that he advances. It then considers debates about intersectionality and the ways that identity and difference are mobilized in relation to discussions about the structural nature of oppression.

Continuing to consider the challenge that Deleuze's work poses to identity politics, the concluding chapter considers the significance of 'recognition' as a key term in feminist debates. Elizabeth Grosz (2002) asserts that feminist theory needs to abandon recognition, given its strong connections with identity politics, in favour of a politics of imperceptibility. As such this chapter contrasts her work with the extremely influential writings of Judith Butler, who turns to Hegel to advance a politics of recognition. For Deleuze, the very structure of recognition is problematic. Instead, political potential resides in the imperceptible, with its capacity to bring systems of sense to crisis. Arguing that Deleuze offers feminist theory a viable alternative to the recognition paradigm, this chapter concludes by examining the rich potential of a Deleuzian politics of imperceptibility for a feminist theory truly committed to difference.

CHAPTER ONE

Thought

What does it mean to think? Who gets to think? What does thought do? When addressing thought we need to be aware that it is far from a neutral activity; not all people are framed as thinking beings. This is particularly the case with rationality, which, historically, has been the purview of white, adult men at the exclusion of others. Notably, the Enlightenment positioned rationality as one of the markers of the human. This means that when women and others are excluded from rationality they are also relegated to the position of the less-than-human. This chapter examines the gendering of thought and the discourses, inherited from the Enlightenment, that have most contributed to this. It begins from our contemporary situation with the place of women in the discipline of Philosophy. Questioning what it is in our philosophical heritage that has led us to this situation, this chapter then turns to the epistemological frames which have refused women the role of rational thinker: liberal humanism and the Cartesian separation of mind and body, which correlates masculinity with the mind and with thinking and women with the devalued body. This book positions feminism as an invaluable tool for critiquing liberal humanism and the masculine purchase on reason. This is not only because feminist theory demonstrates that, as Rosi Braidotti suggests, 'women do think. Think they do and think they have from time immemorial' (1991: 275). But it is also because the historical emergence of feminism runs parallel to a broader critique of the exclusions inherent in the liberal humanist framework and embodied in the figure of Enlightenment man.

Deleuze is an extremely useful ally for feminists committed to challenging liberal humanism. His work offers a radical alternative to Enlightenment models of thought: he liberates thought from the hierarchies inherent to reason; he critiques the Cartesian devaluing of the body as a passive container for an active mind, arguing instead for the imbrication of mind and body; and he releases thought from the interiority of the subject. Although there has been significant work examining the feminist potential of Deleuze's commitment to emancipating the body from Cartesian hierarchies (Grosz 1994; Gatens 1996; Lorraine 1999; Braidotti 2001), this chapter positions Deleuze's concept of thought itself as useful to feminist theory.[1] It suggests that there is something about Deleuze's work, and the way that he conceptualizes thought, that makes it particularly useful for feminists who want to refute the exclusivity of the masculine purchase on the activity of thinking.

Enlightenment legacies

In one of the earliest feminist engagements with Deleuze's work, Braidotti's 1991 book *Patterns of Dissonance* raises the problem of the marginal place of women in philosophy. Braidotti is not the first or only person to ask questions about the opportunity for women to contribute to intellectual debates. We only need to look at Virginia Woolf's 1929 feminist text, *A Room of One's Own*, in which she considers the relationship between women's economic subordination to men, their access to education, and their capacity to undertake intellectual work, to be reminded that women have long been asking for a seat at the table. This is not only the case in the discipline of Philosophy but pertains to the history of knowledge and of writing more broadly, which has recorded and valued male thought. Knowledge has been formed in a patriarchal world and it has not represented women's voices. The author Jeanette Winterson reflects on men's disproportionate access to intellectual pursuits in her autobiography *Why Be Happy When You Could Be Normal?* (2011). In this text she interrogates the formation of her political consciousness as a female writer responding to a literary history that has largely excluded women. She describes the impact of a visit to a bookshop: 'I had never seen a shop with five floors of books. I felt dizzy, like too much oxygen all at once. And I thought about women. All these books, and how long had it taken women to write their share, and why were there still so few women poets and novelists, and even fewer who were considered important?' (2011: 137–8). It is striking that when we look specifically at philosophy today the problem raised by these feminists – that women struggle to be able to participate in intellectual discourse – persists. To see this in action we only need to consider the place of women in academic institutions in which women are far outnumbered by men and concentrated in junior roles. This is particularly exacerbated in male-dominated disciplines such as Philosophy.[2]

The marginal place of women in philosophy invites us to consider how the concept of 'thought' and the activity of 'thinking' – the cornerstone of philosophical labour – have been gendered historically in ways that have constrained and concealed women's contribution. This chapter suggests that there may be ideological reasons as to why women have had an uneasy relationship with philosophy and why feminists have mounted such a sustained critique of the intellectual systems, inherited from Enlightenment thought, which still inhere in our structures of meaning and value.

The struggle for women to find a voice in philosophy is a complex one and brings together issues that have always been central to feminism. This includes the place of women in the public sphere and in institutions of learning, as well as issues that occur at a more symbolic level, such as the gendering of reason and rationality as masculine. In Genevieve Lloyd's influential book *The Man of Reason* (2004), she explores how reason and rationality, the very models that have been considered appropriate to intellectual work, have traditionally been gendered masculine to the exclusion of women. She writes that the 'obstacles to female cultivation of Reason spring to a large extent from the fact that our ideals of Reason have historically incorporated an exclusion of the feminine, and that femininity itself has been partly constituted through such processes of exclusion' (2004: xxi). Significantly, for Lloyd, this system of masculine privilege not only positions reason as the provenance of men but it also contributes to the construction of our ideas about gender, problematically affording men greater access to the production of sense, the methods of logic and the idea of truth. Simone de Beauvoir also acknowledges the problematic gendering of thought in *The Second Sex* (2011), in which she argues in relation to myth that women are positioned as the other of man. While men are permitted the freedom of transcendence, framing them as active and locating them in the world of ideas, women have been relegated to immanence and the 'sphere of viscous darkness' (2011: 271). This problematically positions women as passive, more enfleshed than men and more closely aligned with nature (2011: 270–1).

The alignment of men with the mind and with reason is part of the tradition of Cartesianism, the philosophical system outlined by the rationalist, Enlightenment philosopher René Descartes. Descartes established a system of philosophical dualism in which the mind and the body are considered to be of a different substance and are therefore irreducibly distinct. Cartesianism offers a constructed system of value, which has problematic implications for women. Man, who is situated on the valued side of a correlated set of binary pairs, is aligned with the mind and with reason, rationality, culture and the position of subject. Woman, who within this system is his opposite and therefore sits on the devalued side of the binary, is aligned with the body and with passion, irrationality, nature and the position of object. This binary structure makes it impossible to be a woman and rational at the same time. Moreover, the privileging of reason and its alignment with the masculine goes to the very foundation of how personhood has been understood, as we see in one of the dominant traditions through which this is imagined: liberal humanism.

Liberal humanism is a philosophical discourse inherited from Renaissance Europe that has had an enormous impact on the way that we think about the world and our place in it. Humanism is a secular philosophy because it asserts that explanations for the world should not be found in religious belief or superstition. Instead, we can know the world through rationality, the privileged discourse of which is science. Liberal humanists share a belief in the values of equality, freedom and the timelessness of truth. This philosophical system places the human individual at the centre of its worldview. The figure of the human assumed by this system has an essential and unchanging nature; it is also autonomous and coherent. It is this model of the individual that our legal and political systems are based on to this day. For example, the subject who votes is presumed to be capable of making a rational and informed decision. The subject of legal discourse is presumed to be autonomous, has an entitlement to the integrity of their body and can understand the system of law. However, the figure of the human that liberal humanism projects has also been subject to trenchant criticism for assuming a universal standard. In the twentieth century, liberal humanism has been besieged by critique from all directions. The problem with this philosophical position is that although it espouses human equality, the category of the human on which it relies is not particularly inclusive. This is evident in the figure of the liberal humanist subject, which manifests as a universal standard: white, male, civilized, middle-class, educated, heterosexual, rational and able-bodied. The exclusions upon which this subject is structured have had both symbolic and real impacts. Liberal humanism has contributed to ideologies (such as racism and sexism) that have been utilized historically to justify the oppression of specific groups of people. This is evident when the category of the human operates as a site of exclusion: some people are protected by its status and others are neither recognized as human nor given full human rights. We see the impact of the specificity of the cultural construction of the human in the history of Empire, in which racist discourses have been utilized to justify the invasion of other countries by Colonial powers or in practices such as slavery, which deprive a group of their human rights and position them as property. This entrenched racism emerges in contemporary debates about the status and rights of refugees. In an Australian context refugees have been constructed as racially and religiously other to the Nation, and also dehumanized through their detention and processing under abhorrent conditions. This problematic deployment of the category of the human also emerges in relation to disability where people who do not conform to the normative standards of the able body and the rational mind have historically been considered less-than-human and have been subjected to systematic exclusions; they have been institutionalized, denied the capacity to make decisions and, in some cases, forcibly sterilized.

Throughout the twentieth century liberal humanism has been theoretically challenged along the identity-based axes of race, class, gender, sexuality and bodily capacities and incapacities. Scholars in ecocriticism, animal studies and posthumanism have criticized liberal humanism for upholding anthropocentrism, a worldview that places the human at the centre of all things and conceives of the nonhuman as a resource to fulfil human needs. The privileging of the human has also been criticized in relation to the animal in two significant ways. First, the separation of the human animal from nonhuman animals justifies human-centred practices such as killing animals as food, utilizing them in animal testing and keeping animals as domestic pets. Secondly, the privileging of the human enacts a zoomorphism in which those humans who have problematically been considered to be closer to the animal – people of colour and women – have been subject to oppression.[3]

The figure of the subject within liberal humanism has had especially significant implications for the way that gender has been imagined. Feminists have been critical of the notion of universal human nature for several reasons. Primarily, the liberal humanist subject has a single model of the universal human, based on the assumption of gender neutrality. Feminists have pointed out that historically gender neutrality has never really been neutral, but has been conceived of as male. In this way the male body and person becomes the universal standard in a one-sex system. Liberal humanism is also a form of essentialism because it posits that human nature is a stable constant that transcends historical and cultural influence. Feminists have been critical of the notion that the ways in which we live our gender is an historical constant because it eclipses how we are shaped by both the implicit and explicit values in our society. The critique of essentialism is particularly important since essentialist arguments about women's 'true nature' have often been used to subordinate women within patriarchy.

Feminism and liberal humanism

The rise of intellectual and political feminism in the twentieth century has accompanied and precipitated the crisis of the liberal humanist subject. Since its emergence, feminism has had to grapple with the inheritance of Enlightenment models of subjectivity and has had to work to refute the correlation of masculinity with rationality. As such, demanding that space be made for women in intellectual life has been an important feminist project. Feminism is an unruly and still evolving school of thought. It is complicated by its dual existence as theory and practice and because different strains of feminism have emerged out of different contexts. Historically, Anglo-American feminism can be divided into three periods, which are referred to as 'waves'. When we historicize feminism in this way we are imposing order on a body of work and way of thinking that has no such coherence. The benefit of this is that it enables us to look at major shifts in orthodoxies within feminism itself. However, it cannot paint a definitive picture of the complexity and variety of feminist thought. This way of thinking about feminism is specific to its Anglo-American incarnation. As I will discuss in a moment, European feminism has its own rich and complex history, which intersects with Anglo-American feminism at various points. Similarly, feminism outside of the West cannot be articulated through the 'waves' that apply to Anglo-American feminism. In Muslim countries, for example, feminism has developed along its own course and addressed its own set of problems in relation to gender and sexuality.

The first wave of Anglo-American feminism is considered to have taken place in the late nineteenth and early twentieth century. Of course, prior to this there had been people who raised feminist arguments, such as Mary Wollstonecraft who, in 1792, wrote *A Vindication of the Rights of Woman* to argue that women should have the same rights as men, specifically the right to education. However, it was in the late nineteenth century that this movement gained critical mass and momentum. Feminism has had a shifting relationship with liberal humanism. The first wave co-opted this ideology to argue that women were fundamentally equal to men and this was largely articulated in relation to contract and property rights. First wave feminists fought against the patriarchal system in which only men could own property and in which women were themselves positioned as the property of their fathers and then their husbands. They also fought for political suffrage, arguing that women should have the same right to vote as their male counterparts. The right to vote is important not only because of political representation but also because it enabled women to enter into the public sphere. The political subject who votes is imagined to be a rational person with political agency. This means that when women were afforded this right to vote they were also claiming political personhood.

However, being granted the right to own property and to vote, although extremely important, did not change the systemic nature of patriarchy. Carole Pateman's 1988 book, *The Sexual Contract*, reminds us of the ubiquity of patriarchal power and its concealed place in the constitution of civic society. In this text she examines how the social contract, the implicit and explicit agreement amongst people to live in a society and be subject to civil law, relies on a sexual contract. This means that while the social contract is about freedom, it is premised on the oppression of women. However, the separation of the social and sexual contract designates the public sphere as the realm of the political and of civic rights, and positions the sexual contract, and therefore patriarchy, as part of the private sphere of natural rights (1988: 3). This works to conceal the patriarchal basis of a civic society because it ignores the fact that the social contract is possible because of a prior fraternal contract between men that instantiates patriarchy at the basis of civil life and guarantees men access to women's bodies. Patriarchal power subsists in all forms of contract, Pateman argues, and therefore contract 'is the means by which modern patriarchy is constituted' (1988: 2). What Pateman demonstrates is that the separation of private and public cannot be sustained and neither can the framing of the private sphere as apolitical.

Second wave feminists felt that the patriarchal oppression of women occurred not only through the inequality of women in relation to legal and political systems but also through more insidious workings of power. They focused on the oppression of women through institutions such as marriage, the family and heterosexuality. The second wave feminists were also interested in the ways that women were objectified and oppressed by the vestiges of patriarchy such as high heels and restrictive girdles. The much-caricatured image of a feminist from this era burning her bra elides the complex interplay between the literal and the symbolic restriction implied by this garment. Betty Friedan's 1963 book *The Feminine Mystique* is exemplary of the concerns of second wave feminism. In this text she examines the social and symbolic oppression of women. She described American women's secret dissatisfaction with the roles afforded to them in the middle of the twentieth century – wife, mother and homemaker – as 'the problem that has no name' (2013: 1). The mystique of feminine fulfilment that interests Friedan was constituted through the ideological construction of housewives as happy and fulfilled and career woman as unhappy, which was disseminated through the media. This text is often positioned as the catalyst for second wave feminism but in addressing the plight of a particular group of women, who were largely white, heterosexual and middle-class, this text also highlights the homogenizing tendencies of the women's movement in this period.

Second wave feminism also emerged as a critique of the liberal humanism on which the first wave rested. Because the tradition of liberal humanism envisages human nature as a universal condition rather than as something that was specific to its social and historical contexts, it was seen by second wave feminists to neutralize the differences between men and women. Second wave feminists asserted the importance of difference to women's struggle. However, within the feminist movement there was disagreement about whether all women were affected equally by oppression. Because second wave feminism occurred at a time of broader civil rights debates, it is unsurprising that in this wave feminists of colour, postcolonial feminists, lesbian feminists and working-class feminists asserted that they had specific sets of political concerns because of their marginalized position both within society and within feminism itself, which were not being addressed adequately. For example, Lorde asserts: 'white women focus upon their own oppression as women and ignore differences of race, sexual preference, class and age. There is a pretence to a homogeneity of experience covered over by the word *sisterhood* that does not in fact exist' (2007: 116, emphasis in original). She argued for a coalition amongst those who were subject to social oppression in the fight for a more egalitarian society. We also see this in bell hooks' *Ain't I a Woman* in which she echoes Sojourner Truth's famous anti-slavery speech to highlight both the subsistence of racism within the women's movement and sexism within the black community (2014). Both hooks and Lorde remind us that when second wave feminism is described as invested in difference it is not only sexual difference that became important but also the differences within the category of woman itself.

The second wave was founded on the idea that women had an essential nature, evident in their shared characteristics, which made them different to men. They believed in making a virtue of things with which women had traditionally been aligned within the Cartesian system such as care, emotional intelligence and an affinity with nature.

Third wave feminists reject the idea that there is an essential essence (or universal identity) that constitutes woman and instead position 'woman' as a structural location within language. They envisage 'woman' as a flexible and shifting signifier and thus acknowledge the ways that gender positions have been socially constructed. The third wave therefore celebrates the differences that exist within the category 'woman' which includes but is not limited to race, class, sexuality and the way that gender is enacted. Third wave feminism is exemplified by the work of Butler, who examines the discursive construction of both sex and gender within the heterosexual matrix (1990, 1993). This highlights the central importance of sexuality to third wave feminism and also of the body, as an artefact on which differences are 'written'. Third wave feminism is pluralized and theoretical. It has been significantly influenced by theoretical French feminism, to which I will now turn.

While European feminism has had its own trajectory and conditions of emergence, this is not to say that European and Anglo-American feminism can be separated in a tidy way. There is a long history of shared agendas and the cross-pollination of ideas and texts. For example, de Beauvoir's *The Second Sex*, published in French in 1949 and emerging out of a French philosophical tradition, had a phenomenal impact on both sides of the Atlantic. Intellectual French feminism, as characterized by the work of Hélène Cixous, Luce Irigaray and Julia Kristeva, with its strong emphasis on women's sexual difference from men, has been particularly engaged with the critique of rationality and the gendering of reason. In Cixous' 'The Laugh of the Medusa', she advances *l'écriture féminine* – feminine writing. Cixous asserts that writing is not neutral but is phallocentric and it elides its masculine nature by posing as universal. She makes explicit the link between the silencing of women's textual voice and the gendered history of reason. Women's writing has the potential to express a different form of textuality because it emerges from the specificity of their bodies. In particular she engages with women's capacity for maternity and their sexual pleasure, writing, 'I, too, overflow; my desires have invented new desires, my body knows unheard-of songs' (1976: 876). In this quotation the body is explicitly described as a producer of unheard texts, which emerge directly out of the specificity of women's desire as it is embodied. The writing emerging from this corporeality is fundamentally disruptive to masculine reason and order. This is why Cixous opens this piece by telling us that she will speak of what women's writing will '*do*' (1976: 875, emphasis in original). She commands: 'Women must write through their bodies, they must invent the impregnable language that will wreck partitions, classes, and rhetorics, regulations and codes' (1976: 886). Similarly, Irigaray's work deploys *l'écriture féminine* in order to simultaneously perform a critique of the phallocentrism of language and to enact a performative writing that might be capable of expressing women's pleasure or *jouissance* (1985). Both of these writers deploy women's embodied difference to men – their sexual difference – in order to challenge masculine systems of reason and rationality, reminding us that epistemology is not neutral.

Enlightenment thought persists in problematic ways in our present intellectual condition. Challenging the gendering of reason as masculine has been, and continues to be, an important feminist project. Moreover, uncovering the ways that women's thought and their voice has been covered over and rendered unintelligible within patriarchal logics is imperative for asserting the ways that women have always been engaged in thought. The question that is raised by these various engagements with the concept of reason is: should we claim that women must be granted access to rationality as it currently stands, or do we need to change how we think about thought itself? Deleuze's work is very useful for thinking about what thought is and what it can do. It is opposed to the conventional understanding of reason and offers in its place a new concept of thought itself. In the following section I examine how this might be useful to feminists trying to assert that women are philosophers too.

Liberating thought

Throughout his work, Deleuze questioned the form of, and the possibilities for, thought. His project is to liberate thought from the conventional ways that it has been conceptualized so that we can really get to the business of doing philosophy. For Deleuze, thought is not about engaging with what is already familiar and, in fact, is stifled by the rational and the habitual. Instead, thinking requires an encounter with difference as novelty. He writes: 'For the new—in other words, difference—calls forth forces in thought which are not the forces of recognition, today or tomorrow, but the powers of a completely other model, from an unrecognized and unrecognizable *terra incognito*' (DR: 136). We will consider the significance of the critique of recognition in Deleuze's work for feminist theory in Chapter 6 but for now we will examine what this idea of thought means for subjectivity. It is through the challenge to conventional ideas of thought that Deleuze is able to contest not only the priority afforded to reason in philosophy but also the rational Cartesian subject as the foundation for thought and philosophy. Deleuze does not refute rationality because of its problematic implications for gender; he is more interested in the way that the concept of thought has come to be limited by how thought is imagined. Nevertheless, his work on thought, and what it means to think, has significant potential for the feminist project of challenging the place allocated to women in the Cartesian hierarchy.[4]

Deleuze is greatly interested in the creative capacity of thought. In the central chapter of *Difference and Repetition* he insists that the way that thought has come to be conceptualized actually inhibits our capacity to think. Thought needs to go through a revolution, he insists, like the movement in art from realist representation to abstraction (DR: 276). What we need to do is to destroy the conventional image of thought that has been insidious in our philosophical systems and has been naturalized in our ideas about subjectivity. Deleuze endeavours to eliminate the presuppositions on which philosophy is founded through a critique of what he calls the postulates of thought (DR: 167). This 'dogmatic, orthodox, or moral image' of thought, Deleuze insists, will only hinder philosophy (DR: 131).

Deleuze explicitly critiques Descartes' model of the *cogito*, which is the idea of the thinking self, embodied in Descartes' '*cogito, ergo sum*', which ties the very existence of the subject to thought. This critique is significant for feminism because in removing thought from consciousness he challenges the very foundation of the system in which the alignment of man and mind has led to the masculine purchase on thinking. In *Difference and Repetition*, Deleuze rejects the Cartesian *cogito* as the foundation of thought and origin of philosophy because it orients thought toward truth and relies on notions of good and common sense. This assumes a standardized idea of what constitutes sense and a universalized notion of the thinking subject. Common sense requires a commonality of experience that determines a specific subjective identity, as in the case of Descartes' *cogito*. This image of thought is therefore universalizing; not only does it presume a common subjectivity but it also positions thought, as it is imagined in relation to the Cartesian *cogito*, as ubiquitous. Contrary to Descartes, Deleuze writes that thought might be better facilitated not by the subject or the *cogito* but by passive selves and larval subjects (DR: 118). These forms of subjectivity are riven by processes beyond the control, perception or understanding of the subject. In this way, the self is dissolved into the ever-changing processes that constitute it. The larval subject, being juvenile, in process and incomplete, is more open to encounters with difference than a fully constituted subject could be. In fact, Deleuze writes that thought occurs 'under conditions beyond which it would entail the death of any well-constituted subject endowed with independence and activity' (DR: 118). This subject cannot be the foundation of thought because it is only the effect of other processes; it is the site rather than the source of thought. Deleuze's model of subjectivity cannot be equated with the subject of liberal humanism because it involves rejecting those aspects of subjectivity that constitute this individual such as autonomy, agency, coherence and self-knowledge. This is not to say that there is no subject, only that the form that this subject takes needs to be re-imagined beyond the notion of the Cartesian subject and also the liberal humanist individual that is presumed by our dominant frameworks of political thought.

Rationality therefore cannot be a criterion for subjectivity in Deleuze's schema. Although he challenges rationality throughout his work, the most pronounced instance of this comes in *A Thousand Plateaus*. In this text, Deleuze and Guattari adopt a collaborative method that contests the idea that thinking is an autonomous activity. They propose rhizome-thinking to counter the arborescent thought that has plagued Western philosophy. A tree, with its bifurcating root and branch structure, offers an ordered, hierarchical and therefore rational system for thought. Alternatively, a rhizome, which grows in all directions without a centre, acknowledges the movements in thought that are not ordered and systematic (ATP: 5).

One of their examples of the rhizome is of grass. Here they are not talking about the kind of grass that can make an ordered lawn but the resilient weeds that grow in cracks. 'Many people', they write, 'have a tree growing in their heads, but the brain itself is much more a grass than a tree' (ATP: 17). Instead of rational and ordered thought, Deleuze and Guattari value a 'nomadic' thought that is multiple and heterogeneous, which ruptures ordered patterns and which works through alliance with, and connection to, other things without pattern or design (ATP: 27). This thought breaks down traditional disciplinary boundaries and finds new territories for thinking.

To advance thought, Deleuze disconnects it from the subject and theorizes it as a creative and involuntary action that is immanent in the world. The significance of this cannot be underestimated. Not only does it mean that thought cannot be the property of the Cartesian mind, but, more significantly, Deleuze radically democratizes thinking. In proposing an immanent notion of thought, he counters Plato's concept of thought in which Ideas exist in a transcendent realm. For Deleuze, thought is not the capacity to have an idea or to mount a coherent argument but it is something that exists in the concrete. In this way he attributes to thought an ontological valence; thought is not separate from the world, instead it produces it. This is a model of thought that is self-generating. Deleuze insists that it is not the path from problem to solution that gives rise to thought but instead it occurs through the differential relations of problems and questions. Problems perplex us and lead us to more problems in a continuous cycle (DR: 140). This means that, for Deleuze, problems are ontological; they are part of how things come into existence. An example of this is the way that heavy rain might prompt a river to flow through new water channels. Deleuze's own example is of the organism, which he describes as a response to a problem. In turn, an organism's parts are also responses to particular problems like the eye, which, he writes, 'solves the light "problem"' (DR: 211). This reveals something important about Deleuze's thought, which is that it is not restricted to the human or the sentient: this is an anti-humanist vision of the potential for thought.

Deleuze's work on thought is augmented by his consideration of learning. He writes about learning significantly at the end of the 'The Image of Thought' chapter in *Difference and Repetition* and also, more fully, in *Proust and Signs* in which he considers Marcel Proust's *In Search of Lost Time*. In both of these texts, Deleuze writes of learning as an apprenticeship to signs (DR: 164; PS 4). Within Deleuze's schema, the world is made up of signs that can be thought of as containers, implicated or enfolded within which is difference. The process of engaging with these signs – the process of learning from them – is one of explication or unfolding. He describes the apprentice as an 'Egyptologist' who must learn to decipher hieroglyphs and gives the example of the carpenter who must learn to decode the signs of wood (PS: 4). '*There is no Logos; there are only hieroglyphs*' (PS: 101, emphasis in original), he insists. Interpreting signs is not a search for a pre-established knowledge as a manifestation of truth but involves encounters with the difference that exists enfolded within signs. It is this engagement with difference, with the new, that constitutes learning and facilitates new encounters with, and understandings of, the world. 'We never know how somebody learns', he writes, 'but whatever the way, it is always by the intermediary of signs, by wasting time, and not by the assimilation of some objective content' (PS: 22). In *Difference and Repetition*, Deleuze illustrates his idea of the apprenticeship to signs through learning to swim. In this situation the body is conceptualized not as a whole but as a series of singular points, which encounter the water as a separate series of singular points. Together these two sets of singular points form a 'problematic field' (DR: 165). The process of learning to swim involves opening oneself to the problems that the configuration of these two sets of singular points engenders. Deleuze talks about the emergence of problems in relation to signs. The swimmer must learn to read the signs of the ocean and respond accordingly in order to stay afloat. In both of these texts Deleuze stresses how important violence is for thought. Here thought is not generated by the habitual but by disruptive events that shock us out of our complacency and force us to think. 'Thought', he writes, 'is primarily trespass and violence' (DR: 139). Thought, then, is not about learning a particular method or achieving mastery of an established body of knowledge but can be understood as what Deleuze describes as the 'infinite task' (DR: 166) of learning based on encounters and shocks.

For any notion of feminist theory, particularly as an intellectual pursuit, we need to begin from what it means to think, and specifically, from what it means for *women* to think. Consequently, finding ways to overcome Cartesianism, a philosophical system that has marginalized and devalued women, is crucial. The critique of reason and the new models of thought that Deleuze offers are useful tools for feminist scholars because they challenge the problematic gendering not only of rationality, but also of philosophy more broadly. Deleuze's radical re-conceptualization of thought has the scope not only to change how we think about thinking and what it does, but also to remove the hierarchies and exclusions regarding who can engage in thought and philosophy that have persisted throughout Western history. Deleuze's model of thought has a significant impact on ideas about subjectivity, which, within his work, become more complex and incoherent than the model of the person advanced in liberal humanism.

There are numerous benefits to this reformulation of thought for feminist theory. Deleuze's idea of learning reminds us that thought emerges immanent to the encounter. This means that it necessarily arises out of specific bodies, which can be gendered and raced in a range of ways, as well as having different capacities and desires, and which have a particular experience of the world. Therefore, scope exists in Deleuze's figuration of thought to overcome the phallocentric nature of Western philosophy and to be open not only to sexual difference but also to a rich and diverse range of perspectives. This way of conceiving of thought as situated also has the scope to move beyond the many other exclusions governing Western reason and has significant implications for beings ontologically close to us like charismatic nonhuman animals but also beings that have never met normative standards of sentience: rocks, bacteria, plant life. Thought that is open to this diversity of 'thinkers' challenges the idea that there are appropriate bodies of knowledge and reminds us that the organization and standardization of epistemology is an historical emergence, which is neither innate nor neutral. Thought is not, then, about what 'everybody knows' or about mastery of the old knowledges. Instead thought is oriented to novelty: new ways to engage with difference, new ways to think, new ideas, new epistemologies. Moreover, Deleuze's vision of thought attributes to it a world-making capacity. This is its democratic potential: we can all participate in thinking into being a new and better world if we can become capable of opening ourselves to difference. Despite this potential in Deleuze's work for feminist critiques of epistemology, the encounter between Deleuze and feminism has been volatile. The next chapter turns to the figure of becoming-woman to examine both what Deleuze said explicitly about feminism and also the key feminist critiques of Deleuze's work.

CHAPTER TWO

Becoming

Becoming is what Deleuze offers instead of being, stasis and identity. It cannot be confused with development, growth or evolution because it is not about prescribed patterns or linear movements through time. Instead, becoming is the novelty that is generated when heterogeneous things enter into relation and become other than what they were. Importantly, becoming is not about the point from which something originates or the point at which it arrives. Deleuze continually locates becomings in the middle of things: 'A becoming is always in the middle; one can only get it by the middle' (ATP: 323). One of the examples that Deleuze and Guattari give of becoming is the nuptials of wasps and orchids. In this situation a certain type of orchid, which displays similar physical and sensory characteristics to female wasps, lures male wasps into a strange sexual dance. The frustrated wasp moves from orchid to orchid, attempting copulation and, through this process, transfers pollen between plants. In order to stress that this is not simply a relation of imitation, that the orchid is not simply imitating the female wasp, Deleuze and Guattari describe a simultaneous 'becoming-wasp of the orchid' and a 'becoming-orchid of the wasp' (ATP: 11).[1] Here the wasp and the orchid form an assemblage in which their bodies find new functions: the wasp becomes part of the reproductive apparatus of the orchid and the orchid facilitates the sexual activity of the wasp. This becoming is literally reproductive, but it also produces new ways of relating to things and new embodied sensations. It is this novelty, rather than the identities of the actors involved, that is important in becoming.

In the tenth plateau of *A Thousand Plateaus* 'Becoming-Intense, Becoming-Animal, Becoming-Imperceptible ...', Deleuze and Guattari (2004) outline the continuum of becoming that begins with becoming-woman, passes through becoming-child, becoming-animal, becoming-vegetable and ends with more abstract becomings: becoming-elementary, becoming-cellular, becoming-molecular and finally becoming-imperceptible (ATP: 274). The first of these becomings, becoming-woman, is perhaps Deleuze's most contentious concept for feminist theory. This chapter will examine the early evaluation of Deleuze's work by feminist scholars such as Luce Irigaray, Alice Jardine and Rosi Braidotti, before turning to the less-discussed figure of the girl, which, for Deleuze, holds a very privileged place in relation to becoming. It will then examine the commitment to the future that inheres in Deleuze's concept of becoming, and which determines that a Deleuzian feminism is fundamentally open to the future.

Becoming-woman

Deleuze's encounter with feminism has been volatile and there is nowhere in his work that this is more evident than with the idea of becoming-woman. In fact, becoming-woman is the concept that prompted the very first feminist interventions into Deleuze's work. To understand this fraught concept we need to look first at the distinction that Deleuze and Guattari make between the molar and the molecular, and how this intersects with the related concepts of the majoritarian and the minoritarian. In *A Thousand Plateaus*, Deleuze and Guattari use the disparity between the molar and the molecular to explain why becoming is necessary. Within this schema molar refers to a mass that has sedimented into a stable and predictable state. Molar entities are 'subjects, objects, or form that we know from the outside and recognise from experience, through science, or by habit' (ATP: 303). In relation to subjectivity, for example, this would suggest an individual that adopts an established and normative identity position that is easy for us to recognize. The molecular, conversely, has not congealed into an identity; it remains a vibrant and shifting molecular collectivity. The aim of becoming is to undermine the molar and to become molecular: to find movement, escape routes or 'lines of flight' that allow one to become minoritarian.

The molar and the molecular are closely related to the opposition of the major and the minor, which first appears in *Kafka: Toward a Minor Literature* where it is used to advance the concept of minor literature. This form of literature is not that of an oppressed minority, nor is it a literature written in the languages of marginalized ethnic groups. Instead, minor literature can be thought of as texts that undermine the stability of language itself and of the dominant social order. Deleuze and Guattari write: '[t]here is nothing that is major or revolutionary except the minor' (K: 26). These concepts are further developed in *A Thousand Plateaus* in which they clarify that the majoritarian is about access to power rather than suggesting a notion of statistical representation. When Deleuze and Guattari say that the majority is 'white, male, adult, "rational," etc., in short, the average European, the subject of enunciation' (ATP: 322), they do not mean that there are numerically more people that fit this description, but rather that this figure is a standard for measurement. The aim of becoming is to undermine the majoritarian by becoming minor in some way. Everyone is engaged in this process; the majoritarian is, in fact, an unoccupied space. Deleuze and Guattari write of the 'majoritarian Fact of Nobody' (ATP: 118) and in this way they acknowledge that the majoritarian functions like a normative ideal. Conformity with this standard is available only in a relation of proximity: even those who are grouped as belonging to this normative category do so only by degrees of approximation. Majoritarian/minoritarian is a useful way to think about political structures because it challenges the binary distinction between normative and non-normative (or resistant) by refusing anyone full access to the position of privilege. It is important to acknowledge that differently embodied individuals have a differential relation to power. For example, a person with a female body is further away from the position of the majoritarian than a person with a male body, similarly for different racial identities and class positions. Deleuze and Guattari argue that we are all engaged in minoritarian becomings but that, due to our embodied specificity, these occur at different degrees of distance from the majoritarian standard.

Becoming can only be a molecular activity; there is no becoming-molar. Because man is the quintessential majoritarian figure, there can be no becoming-man. Rather all becomings, those of both men and women, must initially pass through becoming-woman (ATP:

306).[2] Deleuze and Guattari acknowledge that although woman is minoritarian in relation to the majoritarian standard of man, woman can still be a molar entity when she is 'defined by her form, endowed with organs and functions and assigned as a subject' (ATP: 304). They use the example of Virginia Woolf's writing, which is significant not because she writes as a woman but because her writing produces 'atoms of womanhood, capable of crossing and impregnating an entire social field, and of contaminating men, of sweeping them up in that becoming' (ATP: 304). Even the most masculine of writers such as Henry Miller and D. H. Lawrence can, through their writing, 'tap into and emit particles that enter the proximity or zone of indiscernibility of woman' (ATP: 304), and participate in becoming-woman. In *Dialogues,* Deleuze and Claire Parnet elaborate that becoming-woman has nothing to do with the historical category of woman. In fact they suggest that women need to enter becoming-woman in order to escape this historical figure (D: 2). Both men and women need to pass through the becoming-woman in order to enter into any of the other forms of becoming-minor.

On the surface, it is unsurprising that feminists would fixate on the figure of becoming-woman in their critique of Deleuze and Guattari. If we put aside the positive valence that they give to the different manifestations of becoming-minor, we could interrogate the way that the continuum of becoming – becoming-woman, becoming-child, becoming-animal, all the way to becoming-imperceptible – positions woman in problematic ways. For example, it situates women closer to the figure of the child, contributing to the historical framing of women as childlike: less sexual and more innocent than men and belonging to the private rather than public sphere (which is the space that has historically belonged to adult men). It also positions women within closer proximity to the animal, locating women as more animalistic and therefore more irrational and embodied than men. And this is before we look to the problematic aspects of suggesting the position of women is closer to the vegetable and ultimately is closer to imperceptibility. It certainly does not help that Deleuze and Guattari insist throughout their work that they are not speaking in metaphors. However, when considering whether the figure of becoming-women is problematic, it is important to do so in the broader context of becoming-minor because Deleuze and Guattari are talking about women in a structural rather than essential sense. Becoming goes through 'woman' rather than 'man' because of the position that women are afforded within patriarchy – because women is minoritarian – not because of some innate quality that women possess. If becoming-woman was about women's essential nature it would not be molecular at all but rather would be about molar categories and majoritarian frameworks.

The first feminist critique of Deleuze and Guattari is buried in Irigaray's *This Sex Which is Not One*, which was published in French in 1977 (translated into English in 1985). Irigaray does not name Deleuze and Guattari explicitly but she questions several concepts that can be attributed to their work: 'desiring machine', 'organless body' (body without organs) and 'becoming-woman' (1985: 140–1). Irigaray is critical of what she perceives to be an erasure of the feminine and of the specificity of women's bodies and their desires into a neutral desire, which, as with most things positioned as neutral is actually masculine. She worries about the appropriation of 'those unterritorialized spaces where her desire might come into being' (1985: 141). It is interesting that Irigaray would make this first feminist critique of Deleuze's work because some of the richest work on Deleuze in feminist theory brings his work into dialogue with Irigaray's own.[3]

In 1985 Alice Jardine published *Gynesis: Configurations of Woman in Modernity*, a book about French theory aimed at an American audience. The previous year, one of the chapters from this book 'Woman in Limbo: Deleuze and his Br(others)' appeared in the journal *SubStance* and provided a slightly more resolved engagement with Deleuze and Guattari's work. Her interrogation of their work was part of a larger project on the discursive existence of woman and the feminine in Continental philosophy. In both versions of her argument Jardine finds little potential for feminism in the work of Deleuze and Guattari and remarks that, aside from Rosi Braidotti in France (at the time a junior scholar), they have few 'women disciples' (1985: 47). Jardine's point is an interesting one. If we compare Deleuze to other radical French thinkers such as Foucault, a figure of great interest to feminists in the late 1980s and early 1990s, the comparative lack of feminist interest in Deleuze's solo and collaborative work is significant.[4] In the *SubStance* article Jardine expresses surprise at this, remarking that Deleuze and Guattari are unusual as French male theorists in that they publically support what they call 'the woman's movement'. However, despite this stated sympathy for feminism, Jardine charges, Deleuze and Guattari retain problematic gender stereotypes throughout their work (1984: 47). Jardine is deeply suspicious of the figure of becoming-woman because it positions women as a vehicle for male self-transformation. She also points out that for Deleuze and Guattari it is women who must disappear first in the process of becoming-woman. 'Is it not possible', she writes, 'that the process of "becoming woman" is but a new variation of an old allegory for the process of women becoming obsolete? There would remain only her simulacrum: a female figure caught in a whirling sea of male configurations. A silent, mutable, head-less, desire-less, spatial surface necessary only for *His* metamorphosis?' (1984: 54, emphasis in original).

Jardine elaborates her critique of the erasure of women in Deleuze's work in relation to his essay on Michel Tournier's *Friday*, which is published in English as an appendix to *The Logic of Sense*. Appearing in French in 1967, and translated into English in 1969, Tournier's *Friday* is an early postmodern reworking of Defoe's *Robinson Crusoe*, which examines how the stranded protagonist relates to his surroundings in the absence of other people and, notably for Jardine, women. Robinson vacillates between wallowing in a deep and hopeless depression and engaging in furious activity (building an escape vessel, creating shelter, cultivating the virgin land and devising ways to measure time). Initially he names the island 'Desolation' but he re-names it 'Speranza' (the Italian word for hope). Through his mastery of Speranza he comes to the view that the island is a woman. This is confirmed when he looks at a map of Speranza and thinks: 'viewed from a certain angle, the island resembled a female body, headless but nevertheless a woman' (Tournier 1997: 37–8). This woman-island is both mother and lover to Robinson. He re-births from her womb-cave and redirects his desire into copulating with the ground, in what Jardine describes as a 'cosmic orgy' (1984: 57), from which strange white flowers are produced. Of course, we can read Tournier's representation of women as deeply sexist. Speranza's lack of a 'head' is complicit with the Cartesian coding of woman as more closely aligned with the body than the mind. Moreover, this headlessness denies women subjectivity, which is usually inscribed primarily in the face and in consciousness. The island is both the mother of Robinson and a passive receptacle for his seed in acts of (incestuous) copulation that are commensurate with representations of colonization as rape.[5]

However, Deleuze's interpretation is focused not on conventional human gender and sexuality but on the way that Robinson's desire, in the absence of other people, escapes Oedipal configurations and becomes 'solar' (LS: 318): it is, according to Tournier, an *'elemental'* sexuality (1997: 211, emphasis in original). This is because he has been able to escape the self/Other distinction that structures our world and encounter what Deleuze calls the 'otherwise Other' (LS: 319). Deleuze explains that this is 'not an Other, but something wholly other' (LS: 317). We see this through his relationships with both Speranza and Friday, an Indian who comes to live on the island when Robinson helps him to escape from his tribe after Friday is condemned to death. In the transition from master to lover of Speranza, Robinson has found beneath Speranza another island. Similarly, he encounters in Friday the 'otherwise Other', the other beyond the self/Other, subject/object dichotomy.

Jardine's criticism of Deleuze is directed at what she perceives as the erasure of the other in his reading of *Friday*, which she interprets as the eradication of the feminine. Tournier's Robinson echoes what is problematic about becoming-woman – that it usurps female space or at least appropriates it for male self-transformation – when he declares: *'I must consider myself feminine and the bride of the sky'* (1997: 212, emphasis in original). The erasure of the feminine is compounded by the brotherhood of Robinson and Friday: this is literally a world without women. Moreover, with the arrival of the ship the *Whitebird* and its crew, the homosocial world is sustained. While Robinson decides to remain on his island, Friday, unbeknownst to Robinson, leaves. Simultaneously, the cook's boy abandons the ship, taking his chances with Robinson rather than continuing to endure the beatings to which he had been subjected on board. Jardine interprets this child as 'the ultimate fruit of Robinson's perversion' which had 'descended from the sky, not grown from the earth or in woman' (1984: 58). Thus, in Jardine's reading, the child is a product of Robinson's union with the sky and the feminine is made redundant. This world is one in which there is no space for women or their desires only for 'monosexual, brotherly machines' (1984: 59).

The strength of Jardine's reading is that she reminds us that we must be vigilant about the textual place of women and of the feminine in both literature and philosophy. Even when examining texts that are from a context other than our own (temporally or geographically), it is important not to gloss over sexist language or representations of gender, whether these are literal or metaphorical. However, her textual analysis of both Tournier and Deleuze has some serious limitations. Ronald Bogue suggests that there may be more than one way to read the absence of women on Speranza. He offers, for example, a queer analysis of the text, reading the cook's boy as Robinson's lover rather than his child (2009: 131). What is most problematic about Jardine's reading is that she ignores Deleuze and Guattari's larger project, which is aimed at undermining structures of power, meaning and value as they manifest in systems of oppression such as patriarchy. Their references to women and to the feminine are in this structural context.

Braidotti acknowledges that her book, *Patterns of Dissonance*, shares a common project with Jardine's *Gynesis*. In fact in Braidotti's book she recognizes the process of collective feminist research that has informed her work and positions Jardine's text as a companion to her own (1991: vii). Like Jardine, Braidotti is interested in the philosophical place afforded to women within French poststructuralist thought, which she maps against the decline of the liberal humanist subject. Her book, although critical of Deleuze, offers a very full rendering of his ideas.[6] Deleuze and Guattari's figure of becoming-woman is contextualized in Braidotti's work with other examples of the use of the feminine as a metaphor in philosophy. She is particularly interested in Derrida and Lacan, and specifically in Derrida's idea of the becoming-woman of philosophy. This reminds us that many other male theorists have co-opted the feminine in their philosophical arguments. Braidotti's reading of becoming-woman is attentive to Deleuze and Guattari's positioning of woman as a location in patriarchy. Deleuze and Guattari's world, she writes, 'harbours no mystification as concerns femininity or the feminine' (1991: 118). However, Braidotti is critical of the way that both men and women engage in the same process of becoming-woman in their work because this enacts an annihilation of sexual difference. In this way, she suggests, the unequal positions from which men and women start this process, as well as the particularity of women's oppression and their struggles, are erased (1991: 119).

Irigaray, Jardine and Braidotti are unanimous in their criticism that becoming-woman erases sexual difference. This is exemplified when Braidotti writes:

> only a man would idealize sexual neutrality, for he has by right – belonging as he does to the masculine gender – the prerogative of expressing his sexuality, the syntax of his desire; he has his own place of enunciation as a subject. This fundamental opportunity has always been refused to women, who are still at the stage of trying to assert themselves as subjects of enunciation, sexed bodies, and still trying to assert their entitlement to the position of subjects. (1991: 121)

In the historical context in which these women were variously writing this is not a surprising critique to mount; after all, sexual difference was so important to Deleuze's feminist contemporaries working in Europe such as Kristeva, Cixous and Irigaray herself. Braidotti points out that Deleuze and Guattari's timing of the concept of becoming-woman is problematic in relation to the place of women in philosophical debate. It is convenient, she suggests, that as soon as women start to find their voice in philosophy, men want to speak as women as well (1991: 122).

Becoming-woman is the gateway to all other becomings because of women's marginal place within patriarchy. However, there is a female figure that has even less of a voice than woman does: the little girl. In Deleuze's work it is the girl that is afforded the place of greatest privilege as the exemplary figure of becoming-woman. The place of children in Deleuze's writings, and specifically the girl, has not had anywhere near the level of attention that the figure of becoming-woman has had. However, important examinations of this concept include (but are not limited to) Anna Hickey-Moody's work on non-teleological theories of childhood (2013), and Catherine Driscoll's work in which she examines tensions between adolescence as a literal process of becoming a woman and Deleuze's work on the girl as a site of becoming-woman (1997, 2000). Although the girl is not a figure that has had as much critical consideration as the becoming-woman, it is in his writings about the girl that we can really start to see some of the productive aspects of the concept of becoming-woman.

The girl

The becoming-child sits between the much-debated figures of the becoming-woman and the becoming-animal. Like the becoming-woman, the becoming-child is a stage that everyone can pass through in the process of becoming. This means that in the same way that both men and women must pass through the becoming-women, both adults and children must pass through the becoming-child. Deleuze writes about children throughout his work. He also writes about children in their sexed specificity through the figures of the boy and the girl. Examples of little boys in his work includes Little Hans, obsessed with his 'peepee-maker' whom he describes as a Spinozist (ATP: 282), the boy singing under his breath that opens the 'Of the Refrain' plateau (ATP: 343), and Melanie Klein's patient little Richard playing Oedipal games with his train (A-O: 45). But it is the figure of the girl specifically that holds a special place in relation to the concept of becoming-woman. Because Deleuze and Guattari insist that all becomings pass through the becoming-women (ATP: 306), the girl, whom they describe as exemplary of the becoming-woman, has an important place in their work. Before turning to the place of the girl in Deleuze and Guattari's discussing of becoming in *A Thousand Plateaus,* I will examine the place of a very special girl in Deleuze's work: Lewis Carroll's Alice who fascinates Deleuze in *The Logic of Sense.*

In *The Logic of Sense*, Alice is a figure that bookends the discussion of events, language, logic, Stoic philosophy and psychoanalysis. Within this text Alice has many functions; as Driscoll suggests there is both 'paradoxically, a hero/anti-hero in Alice' (1997: 79). Alice escapes the subject/object distinction, is anti-Oedipal, understands Stoicism and, importantly, she is a figure that exemplifies becoming. Deleuze opens *The Logic of Sense* with a discussion of the paradox of becoming which, described as 'infinite identity', affirms 'both directions of sense at the same time—of future and past, of the day before and the day after, of more and less, of too much and not enough, of active and passive, of cause and effect' (LS: 2). On her strange adventures in Wonderland, Alice must navigate surface and depth, negotiate size as her own body and the things around her shift in scale and is persistently required to engage with sense and nonsense. She epitomizes what Deleuze calls throughout *The Logic of Sense* 'pure becoming'.

It is the little girl specifically that is connected to becoming; Deleuze tells us that Carroll detests boys because of their relation to 'false depth [...] false wisdom, and animality' (LS: 10) and, for Deleuze, boys are more closely aligned with molar identity positions.[7] Alice, as the figure of the girl, is able to engage in pure becomings because she rejects false depth in favour of surfaces and can see that the action happen at the borders and edges of things (LS: 9). These are the true becomings that do not pass from one concrete and defined molar state to another but rather maintain their status as molecular. Dorothea Olkowski writes of the girl as a molecular becoming, contextualizing this more broadly with the place of the molecular in the work of Deleuze and Guattari: below Oedipus 'a molecular unconscious; beneath the stable forms, functionalism; under familialism, polymorphous perversity' (2008: 119). She continues: 'beneath woman or even man, the little girl, Alice in Wonderland, releases becoming from the constraints of reference, signification, identity and causation' (2008: 119).[8]

Deleuze and Guattari talk about the girl in *A Thousand Plateaus* in relation to the figure's molecular capacities. Here they remind us that it is not actual girls or children that are caught up in becoming but rather that this is a state that everyone can pass through. This has nothing to do, then, with the ways that girls literally become women, and, as such, female subjects do not have a privileged place in relation to the figure of the girl. They write, 'becoming-woman or the molecular woman is the girl herself' (ATP: 305), and the girl is the 'becoming-women of each sex, just as the child is the becoming-young of every age' (ATP: 306). The girl then is not defined by a particular stage in development, a particular sex, or, as Deleuze and Guattari suggest, a relation to virginity (ATP: 305). Instead the girl is defined by 'a relation of movement and rest, speed and slowness, by a combination of atoms, an emission of particles: haecceity' (ATP 305). This is why the girl is everywhere that molecular becomings appear.

In *Volatile Bodies*, Grosz remarks on the fact that it is the girl and not woman that demonstrate the figure of becoming-woman. 'Not the little girl as vehicle for (pederastic) fantasy or the little girl as pure innocence, or indeed the girl as romantic or representative figure,' she writes, 'but rather the girl as the site of culture's most intensified disinvestments and re-castings of the body' (1994: 174–5). Deleuze and Guattari also write about the body of the girl as a site where potential can be subdued. They remark that the molar subjects of man and woman emerge when molecular figures such as the girl are subject to the 'dualism machine' that constructs masculine and feminine and fabricates a two-sex system of 'opposable organisms' (ATP: 305). Through this process the body becomes not a space of possibility but one that is inscribed in a particular way. 'The body', they write, 'is stolen first from the girl: Stop behaving like that, you're not a little girl anymore, you're not a tomboy, etc. The girl's becoming is stolen first, in order to impose a history, or prehistory, upon her' (ATP 305). Becoming-woman or the girl is about undoing this coding of the body so that girl particles can be released and flow throughout the social field. However, Grosz suggests that in the same way that Deleuze and Guattari mobilize the figure of woman as an abstract figure through which all becomings must pass, they also 'steal' the body of the girl who loses her specificity and becomes something that everyone can access regardless of their sex, age or position in relation to power (1994: 175). Again, as with the figure of becoming-woman, we need to question the appropriation of female figures by male philosophers. We might also ask to what extent the link between becoming-women and the girl infantilizes women.

Becoming does not, of course, end with the becoming-woman or the girl; this is only the first stage in the process of becoming-imperceptible. The pathway of becoming-minor is one of increasing molecularity. In Deleuze and Guattari's work, the imperceptible is correlated with the indiscernible and the impersonal and all are highly valued (ATP: 308). To become-imperceptible is to achieve a state of immanence with the world in which one would no longer be in any way perceptible from the surroundings. Deleuze and Guattari describe this repeatedly as becoming like an abstract line or becoming *tout le monde* – like everybody else or like the whole world. 'One has painted the world on oneself', they write, 'not oneself on the world' (ATP: 221). To become-imperceptible, then, is to no longer be a subject or an object but to be dissolved into the molecular flux of the world. It takes the individual beyond the molar identities such as man or woman, adult or child, and disrupts these binary ways of thinking about identity. This has an impact not only on human subjectivity but also on the structures of power within which we live. Deleuze's commitment to the univocity of being – the idea that all things share a foundational equality – is also a radically anti-humanist position. To become-imperceptible is to disavow human privilege.

What we need to remember about Deleuze and Guattari's concept of becoming-women is that it resonates with the broader critique of liberal humanism that was enacted by feminists, and other minority groups. The majoritarian standard that is evoked by Deleuze and Guattari is none other than the figure of the liberal humanist subject. Becoming-woman, like all other examples of becoming-minor, seriously undermines the stability of this figure. For example: becoming-woman is a movement away from patriarchy; becoming-child is a movement away from the idea of adulthood as the location of personhood; becoming-animal is a movement away from anthropocentrism. All becomings are part of becoming-minor and this necessarily disrupts all hierarchies that stratify power and create oppression.

Feminism and the future

Becoming-woman is the concept from Deleuze's oeuvre that has received the most strident criticism from feminists. However, it might also be the concept that could potentially be the most useful for feminist theory. Because becoming acknowledges that things exist in a state of perpetual movement and flux, it invites us to think about processes rather than static states. Thinking in terms of becoming offers feminism something extremely useful: a way out of essentialism. The notion that there is an innate essence to womanhood, which emerges from the depths of interiority, has predominantly been utilized to limit and exclude women. We see this, for example, in the idea that women are innately more nurturing and therefore more family-oriented, which has led to a pronounced gendering of care and of kin-work in many societies.

Kin-work manifests as women doing the bulk of the domestic work that holds families together. For example, caring for elderly parents, preparing meals and undertaking the emotional labour of bringing people together. This gendered division of labour has also led to women assuming responsibility for the bulk of childcare which has, in general terms, had an impact on women's career trajectories. When we look comparatively at men and women's participation in work cultures the impact of these essentialist beliefs becomes pronounced: women, on average, have less or slower career advancement, less superannuation and are less likely to be in leadership positions. So essentialism is about the attributes that we imagine men or women to possess, but we see its manifestation in concrete situations.

Challenging essentialism not only confronts problematic and limiting ideas about gender but it also enables us to think about 'woman' not in terms of a set of innate defining qualities, but rather as a signifier ascribed to a set of characteristics which is socio-historically specific and subject to change. Because the signifier 'woman' has designated a different set of attributes in different historical periods and cultures, it is not attached to something essential but, rather, is culturally constructed. If we think in terms of becoming rather than being then we need to think about categories like 'woman' as fundamentally open to the future. This way of conceiving of categories such as 'women' in terms of process, change and experimentation has significant benefits for how we understand sex, gender and sexuality. Primarily, it acknowledges the possibility that we might live sexual difference in new and unknown ways in the future. However, it also acknowledges that current gendered identities are not monolithic, and that people are already living sexual difference in ways that we have not yet grappled with in our systems of meaning.

If 'woman' is open to the future, then feminism also needs to be open to the future. Because a Deleuzian feminism is futural it poses a significant challenge to post-feminism. This is a movement that has less traction in the academy than in popular culture. Loosely, post-feminism can be seen as a generational phenomenon. Although it has developed out of power feminism, girl-power and the more radical riot grrrl movement of the third wave, it has a neo-conservative and normative agenda. While it has been described as a backlash to feminism, Ann Brooks frames it as a more positive emergence occurring at the intersection of post-modernism, poststructuralism and postcolonialism and critically engaged with prior modes of feminist theory (1997: 1). However, other scholars such as Angela McRobbie argue that post-feminism undermines the interests of feminism because it either repudiates it or relegates it to the past (2004: 255, 262). This is commensurate with Patricia MacCormack's assertions that post-feminism is insidious, not only because it thinks that feminism has already achieved its goals but also because it is a 'pseudo-feminism anchored on capitalism's "freeing" of women to do (that is, buy and ergo look) what and how they want and, cynically, freeing them from being feminists at all' (2009: 87). The focus on consumption in post-feminism determines that it is a movement that favours individualism over collective action and reminds us of its neoliberal tendencies.

Although there is a propensity in criticism of post-feminism to deride (predominantly) young women and frame them as dupes of ideologies such as capitalism, it is hard not to be concerned by the complacencies that this movement announces. As MacCormack suggests, post-feminism implies that feminism had a goal but that this has now been achieved, rendering feminism redundant. This is predominantly a white, middle-class brand of feminism. As such it represents the group that has benefitted the most from the social change that was fought for by previous generations of feminists. It also assumes that we have already arrived at gender equality. As such it problematically ignores the workings of patriarchy in other parts of the world and frames feminism as a movement addressed to the conditions of Western women only. However, it also disregards the continued persistence of patriarchy in Western countries, which announces itself in the disproportionate number of women subject to violence, particularly intimate-partner violence and sexual violence, the gendered disparity in wages and the predominance of men in positions of power. With this list in mind we need to question whether we are really in a post-sexist society and, if not, how we could not require feminism as we move into the future.

To position gender equality as the goal of feminism is to construe it as a teleological movement that we might, one day, no longer require. This also imagines that feminism has a single goal or that there could be a definitive way to measure its success. However, Deleuze enables us to shift our thinking to be open to what feminism might become if no longer imagined in relation to a definitive purpose. For Claire Colebrook post-feminism is about gender rather than sex (or sexuality) and is fundamentally a gender politics. Either it implies that gender politics has been successful and for that reason we no longer need feminism or it suggests that a politics based on gender has run its course and that we need to think beyond gender to acknowledge more complex factors like sexuality, class or culture (2014: 158). The problem, she insists, is the persistence of gender even in shifts to the posthuman. In fact, she writes, it may be easier to imagine the end of capitalism and of the world itself, than the end of gender (2014: 167). With this in mind she suggests that the figure of becoming-women is particularly useful. This is because of becoming-woman's molecularity. This figure enables us to move beyond man or woman because becoming-woman is not an imitation or parody of woman but is directed at opening up new affects, and new ways of thinking and being. Becoming-woman is, therefore, according to Colebrook, a 'perpetual act of war, waged against the upright morality of man *and* the redemptive otherness of women' (2014: 154, emphasis in original). Becoming-woman is the figure that feminism needs because it shifts the idea that feminism is about or for women to post-gender politics focused on the 'thousand tiny sexes' which Deleuze and Guattari affirm (ATP: 235). The future subsists in the figures of becoming-woman, and, specifically, the girl because of their nascent potentialities. A feminism of becoming-woman is about undermining the fixity of categories and the essentialism that has entrapped women in models from the past. This feminism might release us from the stranglehold of prior ideas about gender or the prescription of a goal and invites us to be open to the unexpected things that feminism might engender.

In the next chapter I turn to Deleuze and Guattari's concept of desire as plenitude in order to examine the feminist potential of their critique of the psychoanalytic correlation of desire with lack. In emancipating desire from the framework of Oedipus, their work on desire takes us to the pre-personal realm in which molar categories like man and woman give way to a complex rendering of sexuality.

CHAPTER THREE

Desire

Desire always tells us things about sex, gender and sexuality. This is particularly the case with psychoanalysis because it is a framework that explains how sexual difference emerges in relation to desire. Historically, women's desire, when understood in relation to the acquisition of what is lacking, has been construed as a great mystery: what is it that women really want? When female desire is understood in terms of sexuality it has been rendered as unimaginable,[1] but also as messy, uncontrollable and dangerous. We need look no further than the closest women's magazine to remind ourselves that women are constantly told what to desire. This is evident in advice and education columns that instruct women how to practise and understand their desires and what products and lifestyles they should consume. Simultaneously, these same media contribute to a visual culture in which women's bodies are coded as objects of desire. Deleuze and Guattari consider the relationship between desire, sexuality and capitalism in *Anti-Oedipus*, the first book in their two-part *Capitalism and Schizophrenia* project. Of all of Deleuze's works it is this text that most needs to be contextualized with the moment of its historical emergence. When *Anti-Oedipus* was published in France in 1972 it was a publication event, selling out in three days. Offering a critical engagement with psychoanalysis, this text disrupts the formulation of desire as lack and its entrapment within the confines of the nuclear family. Deleuze and Guattari's, at times, vitriolic critique of psychoanalysis has significant potential for re-imagining gender, sexuality and family, which are, of course, important sites of political struggle for feminists. This chapter begins with the context of *Anti-Oedipus* and with the critique of psychoanalysis outlined by Deleuze and Guattari. It then turns to their concept of desiring-machines and the scope that this offers for new, positive and non-psychoanalytic understandings of eroticism.

Desire, psychoanalysis and experimental psychiatry

Deleuze and Guattari's treatise on desire, *Anti-Oedipus*, emerged out of a particular social and historical context. It has often been described as a 1968 book, even though the authors first met after the events of May. We can also locate *Anti-Oedipus* within broader intellectual currents that were germinating in France throughout the 1960s. Around the time of the political unrest that culminated in the student and worker uprising in Paris in May of 1968 a series of important texts was published. These works are now considered to constitute the canon of poststructuralist thought and include Foucault's *The Order of Things* published in 1966, and *The Archaeology of Knowledge* from 1969, Derrida's *Of Grammatology* which appeared in 1967 and Deleuze's own *Difference and Repetition* and *The Logic of Sense* from 1968 and 1969 respectively. Although the events of 1968 can be attributed to material factors such as dissatisfaction about low wages, rising unemployment and the conditions in universities (such as overcrowding and out-dated rules), the imperative to overthrow the old hierarchies resonated with the anarchist and utopian tenor of poststructuralist discourse. This is not to say that May 1968 was inspired by the poststructuralist thinkers, but, more accurately, that their work can be seen to have resonated with the cultural zeitgeist. While philosophers such as Sartre were instrumental in their alignment with the students in this period, it is important to acknowledge that many key poststructuralist thinkers were physically absent from the events. Deleuze, who had been very ill with the recurrence of his tuberculosis, was working on completing his doctoral dissertation and teaching at the University of Lyon. Whether or not 1968 was a success is less important than considering the ways that Deleuze and Guattari reflect on this period of political unrest in *Anti-Oedipus*, which is a book that claims that desire *is* a revolutionary force.

Anti-Oedipus also needs to be contextualized with a broader historical situation. Ian Buchanan suggests that we can read

Anti-Oedipus as a 1968 book only if we understand 1968 as encompassing a heterogeneous and dispersed set of historical emergences including the events of May and the unrest that gave rise to them, as well as the war in Vietnam and the situation in Algeria. This broader contextualization of Deleuze and Guattari's book enables it to be understood as developing out of a much more complex set of occurrences that go beyond the local events in Paris in May of 1968. He also points out that Deleuze and Guattari were not *soixante-huitards* but were of an older generation whose political consciousness was formed in the Second World War and its aftermath (2008: 8). So we can say that *Anti-Oedipus* was a book of its time but we must acknowledge that the idea of 'its time' situates it in complex and contested intellectual and political territory.

It is also important to understand *Anti-Oedipus* in relation to the dominance of psychoanalysis in French intellectual life, and the place of this theoretical framework in the work of both Deleuze and Guattari. The psychoanalyst Jacques Lacan was a major figure on the French intellectual scene because of his reinterpretation of the work of Freud in relation to structural linguistics. Lacan acknowledged Deleuze's engagement with psychoanalysis in *Difference and Repetition* and *The Logic of Sense* in his seminar of 1968–9 (Dosse 2011: 187). However, the rivalry between these two men prompted them to schedule their seminars at the same time so that students had to make a choice: you could not be a Deleuzian and a Lacanian at the same time. Guattari's relationship with Lacan, and with psychoanalysis, was more complex and much more personal. In the 1950s Guattari was a devotee of Lacan and trained as a psychoanalyst. He was included in the Freudian school as an analyst from 1969 and he underwent analysis with Lacan on a regular basis. Lacan and Guattari's relationship was compromised by the publication of *Anti-Oedipus*. Lacan had asked to see the book before it was published but the authors refused (Guattari 2006: 343). His response to its publication was extreme: he banned the members of the Freudian School from reading or engaging with it (Dosse 2011: 209).

Prior to writing *Anti-Oedipus*, Guattari had been working at the experimental psychiatric hospital in La Borde that Jean Oury opened in 1953. This facility was founded on the principles of anti-psychiatry, which is an international movement that purports that mental illness is socially constructed and is used to demarcate 'normal' and 'abnormal' behaviours. Moreover, La Borde was committed to institutional psychotherapy, which is the practice of interrogating how a particular institution functions: how its component parts relate, what its investments are, how power circulates and what its effect is on individuals. The point of this analysis is to find new ways for the institution to operate; in effect this is to treat the institution itself as a patient in need of therapy. In France at the time most psychiatric hospitals were run by the state, so the establishment of this private clinic can also be understood as an act of political resistance to the state and its institutions. Rather than sequestering from the 'normal' population those designated as mentally ill, as was the practice of the state, La Borde was inclusive and participatory. The anti-psychiatry movement advanced the idea that those designated as mentally ill were often extremely creative and their 'treatment' should not restrict or deaden this creativity. The clinic was designed to break down the hierarchies of a conventional institution. To this end salaries were radically re-thought and duties were re-imagined: everyone (doctors, patients, maintenance staff, intellectuals) were involved in the day-to-day running of the hospital including cooking and cleaning, and, concomitantly, everyone was involved in treating the patients including the patients themselves.[2]

Guattari was heavily involved at La Borde, where he took up residence in 1955. He was hired because of his experience as a political militant and his capacity to mobilize people. At first his job was to organize activities but he later took on other roles like managing the clinic's finances and participating in patient care (Dosse 2011: 58). Although in the period when *Anti-Oedipus* was being written, Guattari had become disenchanted with institutional psychotherapy and psychoanalysis, he maintained his involvement at La Borde and the impact of his experience at that place on his collaborative project with Deleuze cannot be underestimated. In his fascinating historical account of Deleuze and Guattari's lives, François Dosse writes that what was surprising about *Anti-Oedipus* was that despite its significant challenge to psychoanalysis, and despite one of its authors being involved in experimental psychiatry, the book had little impact on either psychiatry or psychoanalysis and was hardly discussed at La Borde (2011: 215).

Desire had a central place at La Borde; the anti-psychiatry movement was committed to the liberation of desire from social constraints. La Borde attracted left-wing and socially progressive intellectuals and became a place where social conventions, particularly those associated with sexuality and family, were challenged and re-imagined. La Borde's utopian aspirations were not entirely successful. Not only did the non-hierarchical and participatory work allocations lead to predictable inefficiencies, but also the liberation of desire proved to be problematic. In his history of May 1968 and its place in French thought, Julian Bourg uses a story told by Jean Oury to reflect on the limitations of unchecked desire. In a 1984 interview Oury describes a time when he was away from La Borde and Guattari invited David Cooper, one of the leaders of the British anti-psychiatry movement, to give a talk to the staff and patients. Cooper suggested that everyone should stop taking their medication and have sex. This occurred but with an unforseen result: one of the patients died (2007: 174). Although this is an extreme example it does invite us to reflect on whether the liberation of desire is unambiguously good. It is also worth considering how some countercultural practices around free love are experienced differently by men and women. Patriarchy is often still at work in these social practices and sometimes the liberation of desire merely translates as an excuse for greater access to women's bodies.

Anti-Oedipus germinated in this context but the argument emerges as a response to the place of desire in psychoanalysis, which imagines desire in terms of lack, absence and need. This is consistent with the way that desire is conceptualized in the work of thinkers such as Plato and Hegel, and throughout the history of thought. In Freud's work desire is located first within the family, and the process by which it is directed outside of the family is explained through the Oedipus complex, perhaps his best-known idea in the popular realm. The Oedipus complex, named after Sophocles' play *Oedipus Rex*, is used by Freud to describe the psychosexual development of a child, as it becomes a socialized being. This occurs so that the child can become appropriately gendered (as masculine or feminine) and eventually engage in reproductive heterosexuality. The Oedipus complex starts the same way for boys and girls: they both take the mother as their primary love object. A significant difference between boys and girls for

Freud is how they respond to each other's anatomy. When the boy notes that girls do not have penises he understands that they have been castrated as a punishment, and he interprets this as lack. If the girl develops normally she will also understands this as a lack; after all, the penis is clearly the superior sex organ.

What Freud described as the castration complex is the process by which the boy, who at first directs his libidinal desire to the mother (this will later be repressed in the unconscious), comes to understand his father as a rival and develops a fear that his father will castrate him (this fear becomes his super-ego or the part of his mind that acts as a conscience). It is because of this fear that he shifts his desire to other women and starts to identify with the father and his patriarchal power. The girl also needs to shift her object of desire from the mother. This happens because the girl comes to understand her lack as a castration and punishment; as a result she develops disdain for women in general and the mother in particular. She then shifts her desire to the father and later to men outside of the family (Freud 2001). Unsurprisingly, this model of psychosexual development has met with trenchant criticism from many feminists.[3] It is blatantly sexist in its reading of women's anatomy in terms of absence rather than presence and is fundamentally heterosexist in its assumption that the only 'normal' object of desire is a member of the opposite sex. However, we cannot lose sight of the fact that Freud's ideas, although many of them are problematic, also did something important for our understanding of sex. His model of sexual development actually acknowledges sexual difference. This means that he believed that embodying a particular sex had a fundamental impact on psychic development. So rather than subscribing to the one-sex model of Enlightenment man, Freud believed that men and women were fundamentally different. Moreover, as we can see in the *Three Essays on the Theory of Sexuality* (2011), Freud believed in women's sexual desire and their capacity for pleasure.

Lacan (1977) reinterprets the Oedipus complex in order to consider how the child develops a sense of self or subjectivity (which, Lacan insists, is only an illusion) and enters into the symbolic order, or realm of language. We see this in his attachment of power not to the anatomy of men (the penis) but through designating the phallus as a symbolic marker of power within patriarchy. As an infant, the child has no understanding of itself as an entity that is distinct from its surroundings, and experiences the world as plenitude without lack. This phase of development is one in which the infant has needs which can be met by particular objects. For example, the need for nourishment can be met by the mother's breast. As the child develops a sense of self as separate from the mother, the child will also experience a profound and unresolvable sense of loss. The child will begin making linguistic demands both for particular objects and also for the attention (and love) of the person to whom the demand is directed. Because demand is always for the Other as well as for a particular object, it can never be fulfilled. For Lacan desire is this sense that something is missing: a sense of unsatisfiable lack. This lack becomes a structuring principle in language and for Lacan the threat of castration is not from the actual, embodied father but exists in this symbolic realm. Access to the symbolic order, which is governed by masculine power (the name of the Father), provides compensation for this lack.

Anti-Oedipus brings psychoanalysis together with Marxism to critique the way in which capitalism contributes to the confinement of desire. Deleuze and Guattari reject the psychoanalytic model of desire and its coding as lack because it frames desire in terms of acquisition rather than production (A-O: 25). They also reject the Oedipal framework for desire, which traps it within the heterosexual couple and the nuclear family (A-O: 51). The nuclear family, as a particular historical configuration located within a particular cultural milieu, is not historicized in psychoanalysis but, in being given such a pivotal role in the psychosexual development of the child, is universalized. The bourgeois nuclear family (which is the 'type' of family that psychoanalysis takes as its model) is imbricated with the historical emergence of capitalism.[4] Following Marx, Deleuze and Guattari acknowledge the shift from the home being the site of labour and the production of goods to the situation that is most common in industrial capitalism where the home is a private space, which is separate from the workplace (A-O: 225–7). This perpetuates a series of dichotomies central to the understanding of modern life in the West including work and home, public and private, production and reproduction. We have to remember that these separations have traditionally been gendered, with the private sphere being coded as feminine and the work undertaken in the home, particularly around the raising of children, being understood as private. In late capitalism, the nuclear household becomes the locus of the consumption of goods and services, and 'Daddy' and 'Mommy' nurture in the child a future worker who can participate fully in capitalism. The movements of desire become curtailed in two ways within this system: it is enclosed in a triangular configuration of 'mommy-daddy-me' (Oedipus), and capitalism itself, rather than being seen as something that entraps people in certain patterns of work and consumption, comes to be what people actually desire.[5] In this way, Deleuze and Guattari position psychoanalysis as a discourse that fortifies capitalism's restriction of desire within the family.

However, Deleuze and Guattari do not see the family as quite this simple or enclosed. Instead, it is 'eccentric' (A-O: 97), subject to continual ruptures and intrusions from a range of relatives and nonrelatives and therefore full of gaps and breaks (A-O: 97). This does not mean that they are anti-family. In fact they specifically state that it is not about denying the love-attachments or the important structures of care that exist within families (A-O: 47). We see evidence of this common misreading of *Anti-Oedipus* in Deleuze's 'Letter to A Harsh Critic' where, in response to Michel Cressole's accusation that he has a normative family unit which could be a breeding ground for Oedipus, he suggests that non-normative structures do not guarantee an escape from this psychoanalytic structure (DI: 10).

Deleuze and Guattari are particularly critical of the way that the unconscious functions within psychoanalysis. They agree with Freud that the unconscious exists. However, they diverge from Freud and Lacan in insisting that it is the conscious mind that leaks into, ruptures and shapes the unconscious mind rather than the converse formulation. Deleuze and Guattari challenge the psychoanalytic model of the unconscious as a repository of hidden desires and in this way they also contest the model of subjectivity that privileges depth. In their tirade against Oedipus they insist, similarly to Foucault's repressive hypothesis, that the Oedipal complex actually inserts the desires that it purports to prohibit (A-O: 79). 'The law tells us', they write, 'You will not marry your mother, and you will not kill your father. And we docile subjects say to ourselves: so *that's* what I wanted!' (A-O: 114, emphasis in original). When Oedipus is projected into the unconscious it is at the expense of the domain of free syntheses where 'endless connections, nonexclusive disjunctions, nonspecific conjunctions, partial objects and flows' make everything possible (A-O: 54). Deleuze and Guattari credit Freud with being the first to discover these free syntheses (A-O: 54) and the essence of desire in the form of the libido (A-O: 270).

Deleuze and Guattari's acknowledgement of this discovery reminds us that in critiquing psychoanalysis they are not advocating a wholesale rejection of this intellectual tradition. They simply felt that psychoanalysis had taken a wrong turn with Oedipus, backing away from 'wild production' and 'explosive desire' (A-O: 54), and this is what *Anti-Oedipus* sets out to correct. Additionally, Deleuze and Guattari are not saying that Oedipus does not exist but, rather, that Oedipus is not the substance of the unconscious but is merely overlaid onto the unconscious by psychoanalysis. For Deleuze and Guattari the unconscious should not be envisaged as a theatre in which the drama of Oedipus plays out but rather it should be seen as a factory (A-O: 55). The image of the factory reminds us that the unconscious is fundamentally productive. Deleuze (with Parnet) insists, '[w]e do not, by one method or another, wish to reduce the unconscious: we prefer to produce it: there is no unconscious that is already there; the unconscious must be produced politically, socially, and historically' (D: 274).

The desiring-machines

In *Anti-Oedipus*, Deleuze and Guattari advance an affirmative, positive and productive model of desire. For them, desire is not subordinated to lack or need but it exists in its own right. Within their schema it would be impossible for desire to lack because it 'does not take as its object persons or things, but the entire surroundings that it traverses' (A-O: 292). Because desire is not oriented toward an object, it does not register when particular objects are absent, and therefore it cannot be satisfied through the attainment of objects. As such lack cannot be primary: instead, it is overcoded on to desire by both psychoanalysis and capitalism. Desire, Deleuze and Guattari argue, is everywhere and it becomes visible to us through the connections that it makes when it assembles things together.

Desire is not, for Deleuze and Guattari, restricted to sexual desires. Sexuality is only one of the domains through which desire flows. They remind us that sexuality and love do not reside solely in the bedroom of Oedipus, but 'dream instead of wide-open spaces' (A-O: 116). For Deleuze and Guattari desire is not about pleasure and fulfilment. Deleuze explicitly contrasts this with Foucault's position. According to Deleuze, Foucault hated the term desire because he felt that it was imbued with lack (TRM: 130). For Foucault, pleasure and arrangements of power are much more important than desire. Deleuze and Guattari resist the connection of desire to pleasure because their version of desire is not directed at a particular fulfilment like penetration or orgasm, which would disrupt desire's immanence. While for Foucault, then, desire is about lack and repression, for Deleuze and Guattari it is a 'process rather than a structure or a genesis. It is an affect, as opposed to a feeling' (TRM: 130).

Part of Deleuze and Guattari's critique of psychoanalysis is that it doesn't sufficiently account for social and historical factors. For them, desire is not familial, as it is for Freud, but is a product of the social and economic system: capitalism. Rather than interpreting our desires through the symbolism overcoded onto it by the psychoanalytic framework – in which desire is always mediated through something else (the desire for warmth is *really* desire for the mother) – Deleuze and Guattari say that desire enters the social field directly. For them desire invests in a range of collective sites such as the workplace, politics, religion and the family. Because desire is social it cannot be something that emerges from the interiority of the subject. Our desires do not reside in the unconscious waiting for us to uncover them, but rather desire is a nonhuman and pre-personal force, which is everywhere.

Deleuze and Guattari use the dissociative aspect of schizophrenia to explain desire because they feel that schizophrenic delirium reveals how desire actually works. This is not to say that they valorized schizophrenia or naively co-opted the disease into their intellectual vocabulary. From his work at La Borde, Guattari obviously had significant experience with a range of mental conditions and illnesses. Deleuze and Guattari aren't romanticizing schizophrenia as an illness but instead are interested in the schizophrenic aspect of capitalism. In this way they engage with schizophrenia as a process that emerges from a socio-historical context rather than as a psychiatric condition. It is worth noting that many of Deleuze and Guattari's examples of schizophrenia are taken from literature and the arts in which writing or other means of expression can release a schizophrenic flow of words or ideas. Capitalism produces schizophrenia because it elevates market value above all other systems of meaning. In capitalism the exchange of commodities is not premised on an intrinsic or stable value but rather it is a system in which exchange value fluctuates. Capitalism is itself a flow of money, workers and property and it is able to liberate desire because it acts to decode and deterritorialize. Deleuze and Guattari's insistence on the productive nature of desire is tied to their critique of capitalism. They maintain that it is a false consciousness to think in terms of production, distribution and consumption because production is immediately consumption and in turn reproduction. For Deleuze and Guattari there is only production and reproduction. What desire produces is real: 'If desire is productive, it can be productive only in the real world and can produce only reality' (A-O: 26).

Desire is not about the attainment of what is lacking, for Deleuze and Guattari, because it is an active, anarchic and unpredictable force that brings disparate things together. Desire is evident whenever ruptures appear in organized systems. It disorganizes things with its schizophrenic flow, which is why it could never have been contained in the Oedipal triangle. Desire is fundamentally excessive, and because of its viscosity it will always find ways to escape set patterns. It is for this reason that Deleuze and Guattari insist that desire has the potential to annihilate established social organization, not because it is asocial or even antisocial, but because it interrupts socially coded flows so that new arrangements can arise (A-O: 116). This is precisely why desire is productive – it produces connections both between and within bodies, and therefore produces the actual world. Deleuze and Guattari describe desire as fundamentally revolutionary and write: 'no society can tolerate a position of real desire without its structures of exploitation, servitude, and hierarchy being compromised' (A-O: 116).

Desire produces proliferating connections that create constant flux rather than stability. The connective capacity of desire attests to its essentially collective nature because it requires at least two parts to assemble. Deleuze and Guattari call these oscillating connections that desire creates 'desiring-machines' in *Anti-Oedipus* and 'assemblages' in *A Thousand Plateaus*. Desire is elusive which is why we can only 'see' its workings through the connections that it engenders. The figure of the desiring-machine offers the potential for infinite connections because, like the body without organs, it is not subject to prior significances or codings and so it is able to move beyond previously immutable behaviour patterns. These potentially infinite and differing parts and pieces can connect in endless aggregates. Deleuze and Guattari insist that the desiring-machines themselves cannot be interpreted because they do not mean or signify anything. Instead, the desiring-machines are 'exactly what one makes of them, what is made with them, what they make in themselves' (A-O: 288). If we can see desire as an actualization, as a force that *makes* and *does* things rather than as evidence that something is lacking, then desire emerges as a force that generates becoming.

When Deleuze and Guattari talk of desiring-machines they are not being metaphorical. Deleuze and Guattari are not comparing the connections of desire to a machine by analogy but rather insisting that it works in exactly the same way as a common machine. They define a machine as a system of breaks or disruptions (A-O: 36). Desire brings things into connection but in doing this it also 'cuts' into this flow. Deleuze and Guattari's example is of the mouth that connects to the breast, which cuts off the flow of milk (A-O: 36). Here, the initial flow is interrupted by this new connection and is channelled into a divergent course. This image of the machine evokes perpetual motion and production, which is why they insist that the unconscious is a factory.

Desiring-machines break down the usual distinctions between inside/outside, self/other, mechanism/vitalism, human/nature. These dichotomies are no longer sustainable because both sides are involved in the same process of production. Desiring-machines do not respect categories such as the 'human'. Instead they bring into shifting aggregates a random assortment of parts and pieces. They write: 'A magical chain brings together plant life, pieces of organs, a shred of clothing, an image of daddy, formulas and words: we shall not ask what it means, but what kind of machine is assembled in this manner—what kind of flows and breaks in the flows, in relation to other breaks and other flows' (A-O: 181).

Moreover, desiring-machines do not offer a new model of the subject but rather dislodge the subject from the centre of analysis. Deleuze and Guattari insist that the subject is peripheral because the machine is at the centre of things (A-O: 20). Desiring-machines exist prior to the formation of the subject (which may emerge as an effect of these machines but is not required for their formation). What become important are the paths that desire creates: its lines of flight. Deleuze and Guattari are cartographic thinkers. Their injunction in *A Thousand Plateaus* to make maps and not tracings reminds us not to replicate what is already there but to constantly reach toward the new (ATP: 13). Desiring-machines shift the focus from the psyche and the interior, to the surface and the play of intensity. Desire is productive whether or not human agency is involved.

Instead of psychoanalysis, Deleuze and Guattari, at the end of *Anti-Oedipus*, propose schizoanalysis. They describe this as a materialist psychiatry, reminding us of the importance of both Freud and Marx to this programme. The first task of schizoanalysis is destructive: to destroy Oedipus. This demolition of Oedipus is required so that the real workings of desire can be exposed. When the Oedipus complex is at work, it not only channels desire into a certain configuration but ultimately it represses desiring production. Deleuze and Guattari believe that desire is inherently molecular but that the Oedipus complex has corralled it into molar formations. The positive (and practical) task of schizoanalysis is to discover how molecular desire works to construct desiring-machines once it is freed from the established patterns of Oedipal desire. The questions of schizoanalysis, Deleuze and Guattari write, is 'What drives your own desiring-machines? What is their functioning? What are the syntheses into which they enter and operate? What use do you make of them, in all the transitions that extend from the molecular to the molar and inversely, and that constitute the cycle whereby the unconscious, remaining a subject, produces and reproduces itself? (A-O: 290–1). This involves dismantling the ego, and moving beyond the notion of identity. Schizoanalysis does not discover latent meaning in the unconscious. As we have already seen, the unconscious is not imbued with intrinsic meaning (A-O: 180). Desiring-machines take us away from models of latency and depth, and from the 'dirty little secret' of Oedipus.

Eroticism

Deleuze and Guattari's critique of how desire has conventionally been imagined is significant for feminist theory because it opens up new ways to think about eroticism and sexuality. Women have traditionally been coded as objects rather than subjects of desire. Moreover, conceptualizations of sex and pleasure have historically been phallocentric. *Anti-Oedipus* is an appropriate book to mobilize in relation to the erotic because, as Frida Beckman suggests, it is a book that is 'all about sex' (2011: 8). In *Anti-Oedipus* Deleuze and Guattari advance what they call, after Marx, a "nonhuman" sex' (A-O: 294) which operates within human sexuality. Here they contrast human sex, which is caught up with unconscious investments in the social field, specifically with the economy and the workings of power in a particular time (ideologies like patriarchy or heteronormativity), and a molecular sexuality, which occurs beneath the level of the human person. In this way, even human sex is opened onto the nonhuman and eroticism can be released from anthropomorphism. Desire is itself molecular and operates through micro processes. In assembling desiring-machines out of parts and pieces (a hand, a thigh, some cloth, a light breeze, the midday sunshine, a fleeting memory) desire is always concerned with compositions that have nothing to do with the large aggregates of man and woman. Deleuze and Guattari are critical of Freud's focus on masculine sexuality because they feel he arrives at a one-sex model. For Freud, both masculinity and femininity are defined in relation to the lack that women embody through castration, which effectively renders the feminine as absence (A-O: 295). It is not enough, Deleuze and Guattari insist, to expand this model to a two-sex system because the desiring-machines bring parts and pieces together in aggregates that pay no attention to the molar identity categories that this would require. Instead, desiring-machines enact a 'microscopic transsexuality' (A-O: 295) in which far stranger, non-anthropomorphic nuptials take place. 'Making love', they write, 'is not just becoming as one, or even two, but becoming as a hundred thousand. Desiring-machines or the nonhuman sex: not one or even two sexes, but n sexes' (A-O: 296). Here they reject not only the Freudian one-sex system but also the male/female dyadic notion of sex in favour of an unquantifiable number of sexes.

When Deleuze and Guattari say that sexuality is everywhere, they mean this literally (A-O: 293). It is sexual energy that fuels the desiring-machines, bringing things together (A-O: 291). It is for this reason that they say that sexuality and the desiring-machines are one and the same (A-O: 294). For Deleuze and Guattari when the libido is in its pure state it flows freely. However they also tell us that the desire we experience is social because it has been channelled by social, economic and political forces such as capitalism. It is because desire is repressed and corralled that the libido manifests itself through the units that we are familiar with such as the person, the couple, the family or particular objects (A-O: 293). We might feel that we freely choose a particular object or person as the destination of our desires but this occurs on a field that is social, historical and biological (A-O: 293). Here the person, couple, family or object is a point through which desire passes rather than being its final or proper destination. Even when Deleuze and Guattari write about love, they do not frame it as something that involves persons. They write of an impersonal love, which 'depersonalises' the participants (ATP: 40). However, this is not to suggest that love and desire are not specific only that they are not concerned with identity at the level of the subject. They write of the way that the love relation is one in which the multiplicities of the lover are engaged by the similarly complex multiplicity of the beloved in '[h]eavenly nuptials, multiplicities of multiplicities' (ATP: 39–40). Michael Hardt, who is working toward a political concept of love, makes use of Deleuze and Guattari's idea of love as something both nonsubjective and machinic. He writes:

> To love someone, then, has a kind of mechanical character, in that your multiplicities and my multiplicities are able to form compositions that are always both below and above the level of the individual: the fragile curve of your lips with the calluses of my hands, the sea scent of your breath with the earth tones of my skin, your airy dreams of nomadic flight and my terrestrial domestic habits. (2012: 7)

Deleuze and Guattari's work on desire and sexuality is not, then, about the subject/object relation. Instead the erotic is formed out of a range of parts, which pay no heed to the organization of persons. This means that the conventional roles attributed to men and women in relation to desire cannot be sustained. The idea of n sexes and the workings of desire that subsist beneath the level of the person move beyond the psychoanalytic psycho-sexual production of sexual difference through castration. In one of their more overtly feminist comments they write: 'The Women's Liberation Movement are correct in saying: We are not castrated, so you get fucked' (A-O: 61). Deleuze and Guattari reject the central role afforded to castration in psychoanalysis because they believe that the unconscious does not 'discover' castration but that this only manifests because psychoanalysis puts this idea into our heads (A-O: 60). It is only anthropomorphic sexuality that is founded on castration and this has no place in the microscopic transsexuality of nonhuman sex (A-O: 295). Castration is central to the coding of lack in psychoanalysis. Because Deleuze and Guattari's desiring-machines are composed of partial objects that do not belong to a prior whole, they cannot lack anything. Moreover, the phallus does not govern Deleuze and Guattari's concept of desire as it does for Lacan. This is extremely significant because the symbolic power of the phallus is central to the preservation of patriarchy and women's subordinate position within society. Castration is primarily encoded onto women and their bodies, which leads to a sexual imaginary in which women are rendered as an absence and constructed as a passive hole to be filled by an active male sexuality and morphology.

Deleuze and Guattari also critique Freud for subordinating sexuality to reproduction in ways that are significant for feminist and queer theory (A-O: 291). Although, to some extent, Freud's notion of the polymorphous perversity of childhood sexuality is similar to Deleuze and Guattari's notion of desire, for Freud psycho-sexual development is directed at a specific outcome: non-incestuous, reproductive heterosexuality. This ties women to their reproductive function, one of the main ways that women have been subjugated within patriarchy and confined to the domestic realm. Sexuality, for Deleuze and Guattari, does not offer a normative vision of sexual difference or the imagined complementarity of the heterosexual dyad reunited through penetrative heterosexual intercourse. The excessive nature of desire means that it is always more than a reproductive drive. Not only does their vision of nonhuman sex enable a far more complex rendering of human intimacy but it also renders normative heterosexual intercourse itself as a practice that is multifaceted and involves a plethora of components. Moreover, it does so without inscribing greater value onto any one sexual practice or identity, which means that heterosexuality cannot sustain its privileged monopoly on desire and love.

The desiring body is often understood as a topography of erogenous zones. Deleuze and Guattari deal in spatial metaphors and for them love and eroticism enable the re-mapping of territory so that the body can be known in new ways. The relationship between desire and space is foregrounded by theorists such as Lauren Berlant, who in her book *Desire/Love* writes of the 'urge for mapping' (2012: 15) that is engendered by sexual intimacy. This cartographic impulse can be seen when 'a relation of desire creates a "space" in which its trajectories and complexities are repeatedly experienced and represented; and as its movement creates tracks that we can follow on "the body" and in "the world"' (2012: 14–15). Berlant is interested in the normative ways that desire is zoned both on the body of the individual through erogenous zones and in physical space (we can think here of the way that private and public spaces are carved up, and of the zoning of particular spaces as the provenance of a particular sexual public[6]) (2012: 14). For Deleuze and Guattari it is precisely the normative organization of space that is disrupted by desire and love. For them the whole body becomes an erotic surface. Moreover, desire does not have a particular direction such as penetration or male orgasm, and sex need not be teleological. This enables intimacy to be rendered with far greater complexity, beyond the conventional notion that the sex act involves penetrative intercourse between a man and a woman. The desiring-machines disrupt normative notions of a bounded and coherent body because desire is at work in the connection of parts and pieces. Eroticism makes new bodies and it enables us to experience the body in new ways. It is this vision of nonhuman sex that Deleuze and Guattari must have in mind when, in *A Thousand Plateaus*, they write: 'we each go through so many bodies in each other' (ATP: 40).

Deleuze and Guattari write of a revolution of desire: 'For there is indeed a sexual revolution, which does not concern objects, aims, or sources, but only machinic forms or indices' (AO: 366). There are clear resonances here between their theoretical rejection of psychoanalytic models of desire in favour of its emancipation and the broader sexual liberation (including feminist and gay liberation movements) of the 1960s. We also see discursive parallels to counter-cultural practices such as the free love movement. Furthermore, we cannot forget Guattari's involvement at La Borde and its utopian imperative to free desire from social mores. The revolution of desire espoused by Deleuze and Guattari is undeniably of its time. But to render their notion of desire as a mere product of a particular social milieu is to ignore the continued relevance of their revolution of desire and its radical nature. Deleuze and Guattari write: 'the finally conquered nonhuman sex mingles with the flowers, a new earth where desire functions according to its molecular elements and flows' (A-O: 319). Here desire and sexuality become inherently productive. This is not an appeal to the way that sexual reproduction has inscribed heterosexuality with both life and futurity in problematic ways.[7] It is, rather, the production of the 'new earth and people that do not yet exist' (WIP?: 108) to which Deleuze and Guattari's work in general is directed.

Deleuze and Guattari offer a radical vision of sexuality through their concept of desire. I would go so far as to say that the erotic *is* Deleuzian; he is the thinker who enables us to overcome psychoanalysis and the damaging and gendered correlation of desire with lack. Additionally, his work with Guattari offers scope for desire to be emancipated from established patterns. The erotic is full of lines of flight: the compulsions, attachments and practices that escape prescriptive and normative ideas about sex. Desire is excessive and disorganizes things. It is precisely for this reason that it cannot be about identity or coherence. Rather, for Deleuze and Guattari, desire acknowledges the way that sexuality and eroticism are elastic, shift and mutate over time, overcomes the human and always maintains revolutionary potential.

Deleuze and Guattari's rendering of desire as a force that facilitates the formation of assemblages or desiring machines resonates with how Deleuze theorizes the body. In this section we have been examining how Deleuze and Guattari's critique of desire is useful for conceiving of eroticism, and the significance, particularly for women, of rejecting lack, castration and the correlation of sexual intercourse with reproduction. The next chapter will look more closely at the specificity of bodies in relation to sex, gender and sexuality and how Deleuze's work intersects with dominant feminist frameworks for thinking about sexual difference. It then turns to Deleuze's work on the body itself in which he challenges the Cartesian devaluing of the body and offers great potential for theorizing non-normative bodies.

CHAPTER FOUR

Bodies

Deleuze radically challenges the conventional understanding of what bodies are and how they are socially organized into the sexed categories of 'man' and 'woman'. At its most basic, sexual difference is the idea that male and female bodies are fundamentally different: they have different morphologies, capacities and embodied relations to the world. The appeal to sexual difference refuses a one-sex model of the body and therefore it does nothing less than challenge the idea of a singular or universal humanity. Moira Gatens, in her important early critique of the sex/gender distinction puts this really well. 'Concerning the neutrality of the body', she writes, 'let me be explicit, there is no neutral body, there are at least two kinds of bodies: the male and the female body' (1996: 8). Feminist theory has long grappled with sexual difference. This is especially the case in French feminism, where the differences specific to women's bodies and, following from this, their thinking and writing, are used to argue for a positive essentialism. Within feminist theory, engagements with difference hinge on the extent to which the specificity of the sexed body or, sexual difference, should be taken into account when considering the biological, social or symbolic roles or men and women. If feminist theory is about how we live and imagine ourselves as existing in a society composed of bodies of (at least) two different types, then the problem of sexual difference needs to be at the very heart of feminist theory.

However, Deleuze does more than challenge our understanding of how bodies are organized. He also reconceptualizes the body in ways that defy its paradigmatic place in Western philosophy. Most significantly, he rescues the body from the mind/body dualism of Descartes, discussed previously in Chapter 1. Within the Cartesian system the body is positioned at the devalued and passive shell for the active mind. Because mind/body dualism has been complicit in the alignment of women with the body, it has resulted in the marginalization of women. We see evidence of women's closer alignment with the body in the long-standing association of women with nature and with the animal. Women's embodied capacity to bear children means that historically their domain has been the private sphere where they have dealt with the immanent conditions of living such as nurturing other bodies, while men have moved in the public sphere and been permitted into the transcendent world of ideas. Moreover, the fact that women are more likely than men to be evaluated in terms of their physical attributes suggests that women are more susceptible to the correlation of appearance with value. Because this problematic alignment persists in the present day, challenging the devaluing of the body in dualist thinking is an important project for philosophers who want to find better ways to think about the materiality of sexual difference. In order to find a non-dualist concept of embodiment, Deleuze turns to Spinoza. In challenging Cartesianism through a philosophical monism, Spinoza overcomes the oppositional structure of Descartes' system by insisting that all things (God and nature, mind and body) are composed of a single, indivisible substance and as such neither mind nor body can occupy a privileged position. It is because of Deleuze's adoption of Spinoza's position and his development, with Guattari, of the idea of the 'body without organs' that his work on the body has already been so enthusiastically taken up by feminist theorists. In many ways this feminist interest in Deleuze's work on the body is unsurprising: he offers new and exciting ways to think about how we exist materially and this can only be useful to feminists who want to re-evaluate the body and its place in Western philosophy.

This chapter starts with the organization of bodies and the materiality of sexual difference before examining Deleuze's writing about the body itself. It does so first by looking at the sex/gender distinction, which is the dominant paradigm through which sexual difference is understood in Anglo-American feminism. It then turns to the force of sexual difference itself, which has been important to European traditions of feminist work.[1] The final section examines Deleuze's most pertinent work on the body. It argues that his conception of the body is particularly useful for considering embodied difference and non-normative bodies. Because feminists need to consider the many and varied ways that difference is embodied, this chapter concludes with an examination of how Deleuze's work provides a productive framework for thinking about disability.

Sex and gender

The sex/gender distinction has been a key aspect of contemporary understandings of how we live our embodied lives in relation to sexual difference. It has also provided a way to conceptualize the relationship between materiality and culture, where sex is aligned with the body and gender with the way in which bodies are socially organized and lived. Gender, rather than sex, has often been a focal point for feminists. This may be because gender is believed to be mutable rather than fixed. If gender is culturally constructed, then it has the capacity to be constructed differently and therefore could enable us to find new and more egalitarian ways for gender to function in society. We can see the idea that gender identity is a social construction rather than an innate property of an interior self in de Beauvoir's revolutionary claim in *The Second Sex* that women are 'made' not 'born' (2011: 293). This idea has profound consequences for feminism because it challenges any claim to an authentic female essence that feminism might represent. As addressed in Chapter 2, when we look at the vast diversity of gendered practices across cultures and throughout history, as well as the variety of its manifestations in the one culture, it is obvious that gendered behaviours are not essential. De Beauvoir's claim asserts that the relationship between the biologically sexed body and the manifestation of gender is, in some ways, arbitrary. Although a body that is sexed female would most likely express social ideals about femininity, what constitutes this femininity is contingent. This understanding of sex and gender positions sex as a biological and natural constant and gender as a cultural overlay. In this way it reinscribes the assumed disjuncture between the body and consciousness and suggests a causal relationship between the sexed body and gender identity (for example, a female body will manifest a feminine subject).

This is a distinction that Judith Butler critiques in her analysis of the discursive aspects of the body itself. Butler theorizes that gender is performative, claiming that gendered subjectivity is constituted through the repetition of 'acts and gestures, articulated and enacted desires' (1990: 136) that create the illusion of an interior gendered self. For Butler this means that gender, and the social organization of bodies, is not natural or inevitable but a product of repeated acts, which are rendered sensible through discursive regimes.[2] In *Bodies that Matter*, in which this hypothesis is elaborated, she argues that it is not only gender that is constituted through corporeal repetitions. The body also emerges through these processes (as sexed male or female). For Butler, then, the body is a discursive site. She asserts that sex is always posited after gender and therefore we cannot access a body that is not always already encultured. In this way the regulatory system that produces gender positions is also the same system through which the body appears to us (1993: x). The body materializes therefore as an effect of power, which works through regulatory ideals within a two-sex system. Butler mobilizes Foucault to argue that gender is a normative and 'regulatory ideal' which 'produces the bodies it governs' (1993: xi). Moreover, this regulation of bodies occurs in order to maintain the monopoly on 'naturalness' afforded to reproductive heterosexuality.[3]

Butler acknowledges that there is great diversity in sexual morphology. In her work gender is always troubled by those bodies who do not conform to the male/female binary or that undermine it in some way, including people who are intersex, transgendered, transsexual or genderqueer. As such she challenges not only the idea that gender is innate and immutable, but that sex is as well. However, for Butler, materiality is always subject to discourse. While gender regulation is a compulsory system, this is not to say that resistance to the governing norms is impossible. Butler insists that performativity already contains the possibility of resistance because we can challenge the 'naturalness' of these norms through repeating them in a subversive fashion (1993: 181). However, this resistance is possible only in relation to the norms that govern materiality and the iterative practices through which gender materializes. So although Butler's work does not simply reinstate the culture/nature binary and its correlation with the mind/body distinction, her emphasis on discursive regimes does diminish the troubling power of materiality and material difference. The problem with this is that it reduces the force of the materiality of the body, which, although subject to cultural norms, is never reduced to them.

Gatens is critical of the sex/gender distinction and its place in feminist theory. Her work can be contextualized with Grosz's project of corporeal feminism, which, after diagnosing the problematic place of the body in Western systems of thought, searches for new ways to positively re-value corporeality.[4] Gatens is very concerned by an uncritical and utopian focus on gender in feminist theory but acknowledges that part of the appeal of gender is that it quarantines us from the risks associated with biological determinism or the much-criticized notion of biology as destiny (1996: 4). In 1983 she critiqued both the premise that the connection between sex and gender is arbitrary and also the way that this positions the mind as a docile location for the inscription of gender and the body as the 'passive mediator' of this inscription (1996: 4). Gatens is writing against the neutralization of sexual difference that is possible in the framing of gender as a social construction. In opposition to this she writes: '[m]asculinity and femininity as forms of sex-appropriate behaviours are manifestations of a historically based, culturally shared phantasy about male and female biologies, and as such sex and gender are not arbitrarily connected' (1996: 13). We live our biology in a context that is both social and historical and as such the categories of sex and gender, nature and culture are necessarily cross-contaminated.

Gatens's task is also to challenge the mind/body dualism that subsists in the correlation of sex with biology and gender with consciousness. She is committed to a re-evaluation of the body in metaphysics as well as in moral, social and political philosophy. It follows that her work considers both embodied life in its sexed specificity, as well as the larger structure to which this individual belongs: the body politic. She advances the importance of imaginary bodies – bodies constructed through complex and multiple social imaginaries. In this way Gatens both acknowledges the foundational importance of fleshy corporeality and the way in which this body is lived, while simultaneously affirming the existence of the imaginary body and the ways that bodies are shaped by social and historical forces (1996). This is not a linguistic reading of the body so much as an assertion that the body and the mind (or sex and gender) are co-imbricated; the body cannot be understood as mute flesh waiting for cultural inscription but neither can the mind be understood as pure ideality. Challenging the separation of mind and body, culture and nature enables a re-valuing of the body and of the feminine. This enacts a shift from considering subjectivity exclusively in terms of consciousness, to understanding it in terms of, what Rosi Braidotti describes as, its 'embedded and embodied' nature (2011: 4). To understand the body in this way is to account for the specificity of the body and to focus on the lived practices that reveal the various ways in which subjects are embodied, located and connected.

The work of feminists like Grosz, Gatens and Braidotti reminds us that we need to think beyond gender and remember the sexed specificity of the body itself. Braidotti suggests that this is a project of thinking 'sexual difference as a positive force' (2011: 38). Deleuze is an excellent resource for this undertaking because he is less interested in the social codings of gender than in acknowledging a richer and more complex rendering of embodied life. This is not a mute body on which gender can be overlaid or which is only accessible through cultural ideals of gender. Instead the materiality of the body needs to be understood as a force that also shapes how we live in the world.

Sexual difference

Deleuze's work offers an alternative understanding of sexual difference, which does not lend itself to the sex/gender distinction. Instead of sex and gender he writes of the 'intensive germinal flow' (A-O: 162) of biology, which gets organized in a range of ways. This is extremely important because, as Claire Colebrook reminds us, '[d]ifference is *sexual*, rather than gendered' (2014: 17, emphasis in original). It is not gender that produces difference but sex itself. This is because sexual difference is the generative mechanism through which infinitely different genetic combinations are produced and new bodies come into the world.

Instead of considering how sexed bodies are subject to cultural organization, Deleuze and Guattari want to uncover how we arrived at sexual difference as a means for organizing bodies in the first place. To this end they are engaged in writing a 'universal history' (A-O: 139), but it can only be a 'history of contingencies' (A-O: 140) rather than a narrative of natural emergences or inevitabilities. This is a diachronic project because they are less interested in the synchronic organization of bodies than how sexual difference came to be the mechanism for this organization. Their understanding of sex, gender and sexuality emerges out of the interrelated critique of capitalism, the Oedipal family structure, kinship relations and conventional understandings of subjectivity, which can be found in *Anti-Oedipus*. Here they argue that sexual difference is *produced* within the fields of race and culture (A-O: 85), which means that sexual difference follows from racial difference. Deleuze and Guattari theorize the social emergence of sexual difference by setting their ideas at odds with Lévi-Strauss's work on kinship. Lévi-Strauss asserts that sexual difference emerges in relation to the exchange of women and the prohibition of incest. Here he positions the child's incestuous desire for the mother as the primary desire that must be repressed in order for culture to function and kinship to exist. In this way, it is those bodies that an individual is prohibited from having sex with that structure kinship. Through marriage, by which women are exchanged and alliances are formed between tribes, 'woman' becomes a position within a system rather than being an innate modality of being (1969). Rather than adopting Lévi-Strauss's notion of primary incest, Deleuze and Guattari suggest that incestuous desire is created through its repression and that the prohibition of incest cannot be universal (A-O: 161).

For Deleuze and Guattari, the production of gendered subjects within the nuclear family does not occur through structures of exchange or incest prohibition. Instead, the social organization of bodies is, in fact, far more arbitrary. They illustrate this though the distinction between three modes of social organization or regimes: primitive and territorial, despotic and capitalist. In what Deleuze and Guattari describe as 'primitive' societies there are first infinite flows of 'women and children, flows of herds and seed, sperm flows, flows of shit, menstrual flows' (A-O: 142). Bodies are initially organized genetically into tribes and from here they are distributed in relation to social codes (things as diverse as tattooing, singing, myth). Social codes endeavour to organize or territorialize these excessive germinal flows in order to produce the socius. When we arrive at capitalism the organization of bodies in relation to social codes no longer makes sense. In this economic system in which exchange value is variable due to the abstraction of price, codes are not fixed and neither are patterns of exchange. As we saw in Chapter 3, within capitalism, the family, and particularly the gendered roles within the family structure, emerges through a specific relation to Oedipus, which organizes desire into a particular pattern. Shifts in the organization of bodies between the primitive, despotic and capitalist regimes tell us that their current arrangement is socio-historically specific and therefore subject to potential reconfigurations. Gendered roles within society are a manifestation of particular social and economic structures and cannot express anything innate or universal. Moreover, sexuality and desire are fundamentally excessive and complex. The place of sex, gender and sexuality within *Anti-Oedipus* indicates that for Deleuze and Guattari bodies, which are infinitely different, are merely territorialized into the categories 'man' and 'woman'.

In Deleuze's work, then, the sex/gender distinction is less important than either the germinal influx of difference or the complexity of sexuality. In *Becoming Undone* Grosz brings Deleuze's notion of germinal difference together with Irigaray's sexual difference and Darwin's sexual selection, in order to think about life.[5] She describes sexual difference as 'the elaboration of at least two lines of development, two morphologies, two types of body: a divergent development that brings with it endless variation and endless difference' (2011: 3). In this way she locates sexual difference, which she describes in relation to Irigaray as 'an intractable and irreducible problem' (2011: 81) as the condition for the emergence of all other differences. Grosz here can be distinguished clearly from Butler and her suggestion that sex is discursively produced through performativity;[6] for Grosz sexual difference is primary and, in fact, it is what discourse needs to come to terms with. In this way she positions material sexual difference as the condition that enables difference to emerge temporally and to produce variation in populations. 'Without sexual difference', she writes, 'there can be no life as we know it, no living bodies, no terrestrial movement, no differentiation of species, no differentiation of humans from each other into races and classes—only sameness, monosexuality, hermaphroditism, the endless structured (bacteria or microbial) reproduction of the same' (2011: 101).

Grosz engages further with the emergence of difference through distinguishing natural and sexual selection. While natural selection occurs through the survival of those individuals who are the most 'fit' for their environment, sexual selection enables those individuals who the opposite sex find most appealing to pass on their genes. On the surface this might seem like a naturalization of heterosexuality. However, Grosz is interested in the way that sexual selection always operates in excess to survival (2011: 118). She writes of sex both as a mechanism that enables the species to continue and produce individuals which are endlessly different, but also as being about attraction, pleasure and excitation which she describes as the 'irrational, non-functional, nonadaptive operations of sexual selection' (2011: 128). Examining the existence of homosexuality in human and nonhuman species, Grosz asserts that it is part of the general excess that sexual selection generates (and she aligns this with non-reproductive heterosexual intercourse) (2011: 130). Moreover, the continual prevalence of same-sex attraction and of sexual practices that are not reproductive does not, at a species level, prevent the generation of offspring or evolution. The excesses of sexual selection, which include things like colourful plumage on male birds or the musicality of mating calls, are what make life artistic, creative and pleasurable. Sexual selection also exacerbates differences because erotic attraction is about the particularity of the lover's body. In this way, for Grosz, same-sex attraction is also about sexual difference because it implies sexual desire for a particular type of body (2011: 131).[7]

While Grosz is utopian in her appeal to sexual difference, Colebrook is far more nihilistic. Both of them are theorizing the excesses of sexual difference and they are both interested in the materiality of how this is embodied. While Grosz draws on Darwin to engage with the generative capacity of sexual selection, Colebrook mobilizes Darwinian evolution to engage with the inevitability of human extinction.[8] Like Grosz, Colebrook is interested in life but for her this needs to be conceived of both beyond the human and beyond the organic. To this end Colebrook writes of sexual *indifference*. This indifference to sex is evident in the annihilation of sexual difference through the extinction of the Y chromosome, the evolution of life forms better suited to our planetary future which may not reproduce through heterosexual intercourse, or the eradication of organic life on earth (2012b: 167–8). She writes of sexual indifference as a 'difference beyond bounded organisms' (2012b: 170) and includes in this the 'forces of life, mutation, generation and exchange *without* any sense of ongoing identity or temporal synthesis' (2012b: 171). Contemplating sexual difference is, for Colebrook, bound up with extinction. Sexual difference is what enables variation in species but it also requires a certain stability and boundedness of the organism in order to occur. However sexual indifference brings chaos to life because it privileges unbounded proliferation and does not require continuity. Colebrook feels that openness to sexual indifference, in all of its monstrous and inhuman forms, might enable us to surpass the myopic privileging of the human. Moreover, it could help to overcome the dominance of the dyadic understanding of sex that inheres in our systems of thought (2012b: 168) and the 'moralisms of gender difference that have marked normative figures of life' (2012b: 179).

Although Deleuze has located sexual difference as just one way of organizing bodies that are infinitely different, his work has been utilized by feminists such as Grosz and Colebrook to bring new life to the concept of sexual difference itself. From Deleuze's notion of an excessive germinal influx of difference comes a vision of embodied life in which sexual difference generates the vital difference inherent in life itself. Although this vision of materiality might never be quite as wild as the unbounded proliferation that Colebrook finds in sexual indifference, there is no doubt that sexual difference brings forth a world teeming with variation. But Deleuze is not exclusively interested in the systems through which bodies are organized. He also provides us with tools to help us to theorize individual bodies and the rich diversity of embodied life.

What can bodies do?

Spinoza's philosophy is undoubtedly the most important influence on Deleuze's conception of the body and he repeats a slogan from Spinoza throughout his work: we do not yet know what the body can do (S: 125). This remark positions the body as neither a definable nor knowable entity, but as a site of knowledge production and the location of experimental practices. In his reading of Spinoza, the dynamism and capacities of the body enable it to forever exceed the determinations of knowledge. For Deleuze, it is Spinoza's interest in the body's capacities that enables ethical questions to be posed. When bodies come into contact with one another they express their differing capacities for affect. So when Spinoza asks what a body can do he is inquiring about what relations it can enter into and the capacity for affect that will be facilitated by these relations. Deleuze identifies two fundamental questions asked by Spinoza: what is the body's structure in terms of the relations that compose it? And, what can it do in terms of its capacity for affect? (EP: 218). The Spinozist body is articulated on the two axes of the kinetic and the dynamic, which Deleuze also describes as the longitude and latitude of the body (S: 127). Kinetically, the body is defined in terms of its rest and the velocity of its movements. On the dynamic axis, the body is defined in terms of its capacity to affect other bodies and in turn be affected by them. The capacity for affection is not fixed but elastic: affects increase or decrease a body's power to act (EP: 222). This takes two forms: sad passions result from a decrease in the body's capacity for action, whereas joyful passions are the result of an increase (S: 27). To understand the significance of this rendering of the body we need to look at what happens when bodies interact.

Spinoza's world is one in which bodies form aggregates with other bodies. These relations compose and decompose bodies in a flux of becoming. This means that the body is not fixed as a bounded and coherent entity but is constituted through the connections that it forms. The body, for Deleuze, is therefore elastic. What we imagine as the stable body is only a momentary sedimentation of this dynamic process of oscillating connections. New bodies are formed through these assemblages, which will in turn shift and give rise to newer bodies. This is why Deleuze works with a notion of bodies that are collectively constituted rather than individual. Looking to Spinoza, Deleuze writes that there are times when bodies come together and the arrangement is good and times when it is bad. Good here designates those encounters that are productive and increase the body's capacity to act, while bad encounters diminish these capacities (S: 71). Deleuze describes good encounters as those that are 'useful' because the affect that is produced is agreeable to the body (EP: 239). A good mixture will produce joyful affect while a bad mixture will produce feelings of sadness. The more compatible bodies come together, the more joyful affect is produced. This makes the body more active and enables it to form further connections and therefore increase its power. This sounds very abstract but really it is quite simple and we can look at workplace cultures to illustrate this point. When good mixtures of people come together they produce good affect and are more productive. They may be productive in a way that serves capitalism but this is not what would necessarily interest Spinoza or Deleuze. Rather they are productive of a range of material and immaterial things, such as friendships, ideas and jokes, which could well undermine managerial ideas about 'productivity'. On the other hand we could look at a toxic workplace as an example of incompatible bodies. Often in this kind of environment bodies cannot produce joyful coalitions and the arrangement is less productive. The aim is to get the right combination of bodies. However, we never know in advance which combination of bodies will produce the most joy or how long they will remain compatible. This means that the relation of bodies is always dynamic and experimental.

Spinoza calls 'common notions' the realization that a union is compatible and that something is shared between two (or more) bodies. This should not be understood as a normative notion of the body by which bodies that are of the same sex or race (for example) find harmony. Nor can it be correlated with 'common sense'. Instead, Deleuze provides as the examples of common notions 'extension, or movement and rest' (EP: 276), which are common to all things to different degrees. It is for this reason that Deleuze asserts that the racehorse and plough horse are more different from each other than the plough horse and the ox. 'This is because', he writes, 'the racehorse and the plough horse do not have the same affects nor the same capacity for being affected; the plough horse has affects in common rather with the ox' (S: 124). Here we can see that commonality exists through actions rather than identities or taxonomical classifications.

This understanding of bodies privileges affects and actions over identity, and conceives of the body in terms of doing rather than being. Because we need to understand the affective capacity of the body in particular arrangements, we are invited to think in terms of localized interactions. This notion of the body is at odds, then, with the impenetrability of the liberal humanist subject discussed in Chapter 1, which remains the agent of affect rather than the subject of affective influences. The body cannot be thought of as the origin or final point of identity because embodied individuals are enmeshed in active processes of engagement with their surroundings. By emphasizing the productive spaces between bodies, this foundation brings the body into dynamic connections with the world. This kind of body is networked inextricably with its environment, reminding us of the primacy of the interactions of the body, rather than its form or content.

In Deleuze's materialist politics, sociality is constituted through the mixture of bodies. In the absence of the stable autonomous subject, Deleuze renders the body as the site of political action. Although this locates politics at a corporeal level, it does not do so individually because of the collective nature of Deleuzian embodiment. This implies that the social fabric can be thought of as an ethical space in which we negotiate encounters between bodies. These processes are literally world-making because the connections between bodies produce new bodies and a new world. Although this means that the individual is embedded within a particular structure of relations this does not suggest that these alignments are static. Instead, these processes occur against the constantly shifting backdrop of a world caught in the process of becoming and with other individuals who are also in a state of oscillating connection, disconnection and re-connection.

It is important to remember that the bodies that form connections with one another need not be of the same type. These connections do not discriminate between the human and the nonhuman, giving rise to a complex network of relations between diverse entities. Moreover, one of the most significant aspects of Deleuze's idea of the body is that it is not anthropomorphic: thinking about the body in terms of arrangements of disparate parts need not be limited to the human or even the organism. For Deleuze, a body can be chemical, political, corporate or social; it can be organic or artificial. Gatens points out that this means that 'human bodies are always part of more complex bodies: the family, schools, institutions of all kinds, and ultimately, a body politic' (2000: 66). We need to understand bodies that defy the humanist scale of the subject in this way. One of the benefits of shifting the emphasis away from human subjectivity is that we can examine patterns of movement and stasis within systems.

In *A Thousand Plateaus*, Deleuze and Guattari acknowledge that Spinoza's understanding of the body is commensurate with their figure of the body without organs (ATP: 170). However, the body without organs is first present in *The Logic of Sense*, before appearing in the *Capitalism and Schizophrenia* diptych. This figure is drawn from the work of the schizophrenic playwright Antonin Artaud who writes about the uselessness of organs in his radio play *To Have Done with the Judgement of God*. To make a 'body without organs', he writes, will result in emancipation from the 'automatic reactions' of the subject and restore 'true freedom' (1976: 571). Deleuze and Guattari follow Artaud in their desire to disorganize the body. However, the body without organs is not a rejection of the organs *per se*, but, rather, the organization of organs into the organism (ATP: 175). To realize a body without organs is to divest the body of the logic by which it is conventionally organized and understood in terms of organs, systems and functions. In *A Thousand Plateaus*, Deleuze and Guattari wonder: 'Why not walk with your head, sing with your sinuses, see through your skin, breath with your belly?' (ATP: 167).

The body without organs disrupts the conventional coding and interpretation of the body. Deleuze and Guattari claim that it is what remains after the 'phantasy, and significances and subjectifications' have been taken away (ATP: 168). This means that the significances that are mapped onto particular organs become unstuck. We see this, for example, with the power attributed to the male anatomy by psychoanalysis, as discussed in the previous chapter. The body without organs reminds us that the phallus is symbolic and designates the possession of power within patriarchy; the connection between the phallus and the penis is therefore not organic. The way that the body is organized and the significances that are mapped onto it are important for the emergence of coherent and gendered subjectivity within psychoanalysis. However, for Deleuze and Guattari this is not the case. Because the body without organs is an attempt to find new functions and to form new assemblages, prior significances such as those attributed to the phallus cannot be sustained and neither can the subjectification and coherence that might arise from them.

If the body is actual, then the body without organs is a site of virtual potentialities. Deleuze and Guattari observe that the body without organs needs to be actively constructed but that this needs to be undertaken with caution. The aim is not to wildly destratify the organism, significance and subjectification because this would result in the production of a body without organs that is botched (ATP: 168). This would mean that the intensities and the flows of possibility on its surface would grind to a halt. In fact, the body without organs can never be entirely free of the sedimentation of social coding because it must articulate itself against (and thus exist within) the structures that organize the world. Deleuze and Guattari tell us that when making a body without organs we need to work with a file rather than a sledgehammer (ATP: 177). They write:

> You have to keep enough of the organism for it to reform each dawn; and you have to keep small supplies of significance and subjectification, if only to turn them against their own systems when the circumstances demand it, when things, persons, even situations, force you to; and you have to keep small rations of subjectivity in sufficient quantity to enable you to respond to the dominant reality. (ATP: 178)

The body without organs is something that needs to be made through careful experimentation. Starting from an organized body, the aim is to find possible escape routes or lines of flight. This occurs through finding new connections and functions and producing new intensities and flows (ATP: 178).

The connections enabled by the body without organs reveal that, like Spinoza's body, it is always a collective rather than individualistic project. Deleuze and Guattari write that consequently we cannot think of the body without organs belonging to an individual subject. It is, rather, composed of a range of entities and things such as plants, people, machines, objects as well as bits and pieces of all of these items (ATP: 179). The body cannot be thought of as individual, bounded or coherent because it is constituted fundamentally by the connections it enters into. Always forming experimental alignments, this body has no desire to be either standardized or normative. These connections do not discriminate between the human and the nonhuman, the organic and the inorganic or the natural and the artificial. Deleuze and Guattari insist that the body without organs is a plane of consistency or immanence, formed through experimentally creating new pathways through which desire can flow.

The model of the body that Deleuze takes from Spinoza and then develops with Guattari is potentially of great use for feminist theory. Both Deleuze's Spinozist understanding of the body and the concept of the body without organs offer feminism a joyous and exuberant body to work with. We have to remember that Deleuze and Guattari tell us in *A Thousand Plateaus* that the body without organs can be full of 'gaiety, ecstasy, and dance' (ATP: 167). Deleuze's concept of the body enables the differences that we embody to be considered in a positive way, rather than through their degrees of divergence from a normative ideal. This is because Deleuze not only liberates the body from its prior frameworks and significances but he also offers a way to think about a variety of bodies in terms of what they can do rather than in relation to discrete identities. As such he provides an affirmative way to think about bodies that do not conform to a standardized model. Consequently, Deleuze's work can be used to challenge the notion of universal humanity on which liberal humanism rests. It is when we look at the bodies that are conventionally excluded from, and marginalized by, the normative vision of the body that the use-value of Deleuze's work in this area becomes explicit. We see this, of course, in relation to the sexed specificity of bodies but it is even more marked in the case of disability.

Deleuze's work on the body has proved to be particularly fruitful for thinking about bodily capacities and incapacities. Margrit Shildrick, whose work examines medical discourses about gendered, disabled and queer bodies, and who pioneers the use of Deleuze in disability studies, writes: 'Like the female body, the corporeality of disability has widely figured in the western imaginary as disordered and uncontrollable, both seductive and repulsive, as threatening contamination of those who come too close, linked to disease, and so lacking in boundaries as to overwhelm normative subjectivity' (2004).[9] Here Shildrick points to the cultural alignment of female bodies and disabled bodies, further reminding us that feminist theory needs to account for the many and varied ways in which difference manifests through embodiment. Deleuze's work on the body enables us to engage in a positive reading of disabled bodies because he rejects normative understandings of the body's functions in favour of a model where all doing (including inaction) produces affect. Thinking about bodies in terms of their capacity for affect is beneficial because it shifts the understanding of bodies to a criterion that does not rely on normative standards of either morphology or ability: all bodies have a capacity for affect. This also provides a way to think about the material ways that bodies come into contact and exist in their surroundings. Hickey-Moody finds great potential in Deleuze's rendering of the body in terms of affect for thinking about intellectual disability.[10] Because Deleuze, following Spinoza, rejects the separation of mind and body his work provides a more complex way to engage with the bodies of intellectually disabled people rather than negating them. 'Through a Spinozist lens', Hickey-Moody asserts, 'a body is not able or disabled: it just is' (2009: 6). She emphasizes that disabled bodies (and all bodies) need to be understood through the affects that they can produce and not through medical discourse and its normative standards (2006: 195).

This focus on what bodies can do challenges conceptualizations of disability that figure the disabled body as one that cannot do particular things or that fails when measured against the standard of the normative body. Shildrick utilizes Deleuze to critique both conventional disability politics and understandings of the disabled body. She finds great potential in the fact that in his work 'corporeality is no longer to be thought in terms of integral entities, but only as engaged in ever dynamic and innovatory linkages; bodies are neither whole nor broken, but simply in a process of becoming' (2013: 152). Deleuze's rendering of bodies both in terms of the disorganization of the body without organs and the innovative assemblages that these bodies can form (including affective relations with nonhuman and inorganic bodies) challenges many of the aspects of subjectivity that have traditionally excluded disabled people. The figure of the assemblage is democratizing in that all bodies can take part in such a way that the dichotomies of sameness/difference, lack/wholeness come unstuck. Moreover, the interrelation of all bodies, normative or otherwise, problematizes the capacities for self-control and independence on which the subject of liberal humanism rests. In fact, Deleuze's idea of interconnected bodies demonstrates that we are all interdependent beings. For Shildrick, Deleuze's work provides ways to re-imagine citizenship which are not about the fight for inclusion within the body-politic but a broader re-imagining of the social whole, no longer premised on the exclusion of disabled bodies. This is a society, she insists, in which the ethical imperative in relation to disability is not about dealing with inequality but about acknowledging the fundamental interconnection of all bodies (2013: 152–5).

Deleuze's work offers us a new and positive way to think about the body. It challenges the dualisms through which women have been devalued in Western philosophy. However, the task of feminism cannot only be challenging the problematic alignment of women with corporeality. We need to shift the way that we *think* about the body itself – how it generates meaning, what its capacities are and what this means for our politics. Deleuze offers a version of the body that is active rather than passive and networked in relational structures rather than autonomous. His model of embodiment enables us to think about particular bodies not in terms of their conformity or otherwise to a normative ideal, but in terms of their actions, the arrangements they can enter into and what they can become. The suggestion that we need to think about the body, not in terms of what it *is* but in terms of what it can *do*, has a significant impact on the stability of the liberal humanist subject as the foundation of politics. The question of what the body *is* will interest those who seek to preserve or reinstate a normative model of the body. However, focusing instead on embodied practices renders the question of what the body can *do* far more productive. This framework has been immensely useful not only for disability studies but also for other affirmations of bodies that do not conform to normative standards. As such Deleuze offers us the scope for a politics in which embodied difference is not merely enabled but affirmed.

Deleuze theorizes bodies in a way that is attentive, not only to sexual difference but to the many and complex ways in which difference is embodied. Feminism, if it is to remain relevant into the future, must commit to a politics of difference in its richness and complexity. The task of feminist theory, then, is to grapple the differences that compose our material world. With this in mind, the next chapter engages with Deleuze's metaphysical concept of difference, which positions difference rather than identity at the foundation of all things.

CHAPTER FIVE

Difference

As a concept, 'difference' is generally understood to mean the variation between two distinct things. We can see this in the definition of 'different' in the *Oxford English Dictionary*: '[h]aving characters or qualities which diverge from one another; having unlike or distinguishing attributes; not of the same kind; not alike; of other nature, form, or quality'. This definition indicates how important comparison is to the way that difference is conventionally understood. Within this framework the concept of woman is comprehended in relation to man, as a subject that has a sexed identity that is distinct from the identity of man. However, Deleuze's concept of difference is radically at odds with this orthodoxy. The key to understanding his complex notion of difference, and perhaps his work in general, is his 1968 text *Difference and Repetition*. In this text Deleuze is not interested in a tame or conventional notion of difference. In fact, his aim, and the project that he identifies for a philosophy of difference more broadly, is to 'rescue' difference from what he considers to be its impoverished forms (DR: 29). He wants to find a way to think about difference beyond identity, opposition, analogy or resemblance (DR: 29). This is because to conceive of difference solely in terms of these categories ignores a deeper level of difference, which is what particularly interests him. Beneath such limited framings of difference, Deleuze argues, lies 'a swarm of differences, a pluralism of free, wild or untamed differences; a properly differential and original space and time' (DR: 50). Deleuze suggests that because we have come to understand difference through the relation between things, we do not have an adequate idea of difference as such. What he is trying to articulate is a concept of difference in and of itself, which he calls 'pure difference' (DR: xx).

Deleuze insists that it is this difference, rather than identity, that is at the foundation of being. This means that the politics that we might draw out of his work cannot be an identity politics – one of the main ways in which feminism has been imagined. Feminists have always negotiated ideas about identity and difference. This is evident in the divergent agendas in Anglo-American feminism such as egalitarian feminism's imperative to erase difference, essentialism's appeal to the different embodied specificity of men and women or debates about the salience of 'woman' as an identity category and the foundation for politics in third wave feminism. This chapter outlines Deleuze's revolutionary concept of difference. It then turns to ideas about structure and genesis, or the tension between established structures of coherence and the destabilizing capacities of genetic difference and molecular becomings. It concludes by examining how identity positions are always themselves fragmented by our complex identifications, which determine that individuals must negotiate the intersectional nature of difference and identity.

Pure difference

Difference and Repetition is the text in which Deleuze's own, original philosophical position emerges (DR: xv). However, his concepts of difference and repetition appear, in part, through his critique of the work of others. We see this in the first chapter of this text, in which he will arrive at his own formulation of difference by distinguishing himself from four other philosophers: Aristotle, Hegel, Leibniz and Plato. His criticism of these philosophers is fixated on the place of identity in their work. For example, he criticizes Aristotle for understanding difference through the division of things into sets or categories that differ from each other (DR: 33). This way of thinking about difference is too static and does not allow for how things become different over time – which will, after all, problematize their categorization. Aristotle's understanding of difference, according to Deleuze, relies on the comprehension of prior concepts and therefore places identity before difference and is subservient to representation (DR: 31–2).

Deleuze is critical of Hegel and Leibniz because he feels that they render identity absolute. They do this in different ways: Hegel's difference is infinitely large while Leibniz's is infinitely small. His criticism of Hegel is not limited to *Difference and Repetition* but is evident throughout much of his work.[1] His early writings on the history of philosophy, particularly his work on Spinoza, Nietzsche and Bergson, were an attempt to overcome the dominance of Hegel in the canon of Western thought and to place his own philosophy in an alternative lineage of thinkers. Deleuze argues that Hegel conceived of difference as infinitely large by figuring it dialectically as contradiction, which positions it at its absolute maximum (DR: 44). Moreover, he insists that because, within the Hegelian dialectic, things are constituted against what they are not, they must therefore carry this negative with them as part of their identity. In this way Hegel traps difference within contradiction (DR: 49). In Deleuze's work more broadly he rejects the centrality of negation that Hegel prioritizes in favour of an affirmative position. While Deleuze is critical of Hegel's 'large' differences, he also rejects the 'small' differences that Leibniz offers. Unlike Hegel and Aristotle, Leibniz does not conceive of difference in terms of contradiction (DR: 46). This is because for him there is always the presence of smaller and smaller units of difference, which exist incrementally between whole numbers. These infinitely small differences elude finality and always recede just beyond our grasp. Although Hegel and Leibniz share with Deleuze an insistence on the importance of difference, he resolves that ultimately their positions remain trapped in the logic of identity (DR: 50).

In turning to Plato, Deleuze is again looking to advance through critique his own concept of difference in itself. He does this by reformulating Plato's concept of the simulacrum. For Plato, the world is separated into the ideal realm of ideas, which are reproduced as actual things in the form of faithful copies (good) and degraded simulacra (bad). This is a hierarchical system in which difference exists to distinguish the original from its replication and to adjudicate between good and bad copies. Deleuze cannot accept this version of the world, not only because it is premised on the transcendence that he seeks to eradicate in favour of immanence, but also because of how difference functions as an external rather than internal property of things (DR: 66). For Deleuze ideas are not discrete as they are for Plato but are multiplicities. These ideas do not produce true copies but are differential, producing simulacra. This is commensurate with his philosophy of difference because '[s]ystems in which different relates to different through difference itself are systems of simulacra' (DR: 277). In this figuration, a simulacrum is not a corrupted copy of an original idea but is what undermines the notion that there ever was an original from which it could be copied. In Deleuze's world, therefore, there is no point in evaluating the difference between original and copy and consequently he frees difference from evaluation.

Accompanying this negative critique of the work of others is the emergence of Deleuze's own position on difference in which it is afforded autonomy. Rather than conceiving of difference as something that appears through classification and comparison, he maintains its pure form, in which it is active in its own right. His overarching critique is that historically identity is assumed to be at the foundation of things. Inverting this notion, Deleuze claims that it is difference and not identity that has metaphysical primacy, that is, he writes, 'difference is behind everything, but behind difference there is nothing' (DR: 57). This does not mean that there is no identity in the world; only that identities emerge out of a *prior* difference.

Deleuze addresses the dynamic nature of difference through his work on repetition, which demonstrates how difference unfolds itself through time. In *Difference and Repetition*, he turns immediately from theorizing his concept of difference *in* itself to proposing repetition *for* itself. He had already addressed repetition in his book *Nietzsche and Philosophy* in which many of his ideas about difference germinated. This book stages his engagement with the eternal return, a concept that in *Difference and Repetition* is described as the 'for-itself of difference' (DR: 125). Similarly, to the work he has done on difference, Deleuze's work on repetition challenges its conventional meaning so that repetition can be understood beyond the idea of unchanging replication. In his work on Nietzsche he revises the figure of the eternal return so that rather than envisaging it as the mechanism by which the same is reproduced (the repetition of a prior identity), it is generative of difference (NP: 46). 'The subject of the eternal return', Deleuze writes, 'is not the same but the different, not the similar but the dissimilar, not the one but the many, not necessity but chance' (DR: 126).

This makes sense when contextualized with his commitment to the foundational nature of difference rather than identity. The eternal return exists in a world in which pure difference subsists beneath everything and this, rather than identity, is what gets repeated. The eternal return is conceived of against the background of the competing forces that compose the world. It requires the selection of (superior) active rather than (inferior) reactive forces. Nietzsche calls active those forces that affirm differences and therefore increases the capacity for action. He calls reactive those forces that are passive and negate other forces (NP: 40–1). The eternal return selects and thereby affirms active forces. It is through this refusal of negation that Deleuze is able to recruit Nietzsche in his campaign against Hegel and the negative. Deleuze makes much of Nietzsche's discussion of the role of chance in the eternal return through the example of the dice throw (NP: 26). The good player always rolls the winning number by default because they have already accepted all possible combinations and therefore affirm the role of chance and its necessity. The eternal return is not the return of the same but is unpredictable and experimental. In repeating difference it is part of the motor of becoming as addressed in Chapter 2. Deleuze describes the eternal return as the 'being of becoming' (NP: 24). This means, ironically, that difference is the only 'sameness' that returns and it returns eternally.

Even though the eternal return is what guarantees difference, Deleuze also describes it as 'the univocity of being, the effective realisation of that univocity' (DR: 41). At first this may seem contradictory: how can something produce endless difference but be expressed in a single voice? Deleuze draws the idea of univocity from the medieval philosopher Duns Scotus and augments this with his reading of Spinoza and Nietzsche to theorize a world composed of a singular substance (DR: 39–41). In Spinoza's work this is evident in his idea that there is nothing external to, or outside of, being. We can see this in the Spinozist idea that there is no distinction between God and the world because they are composed of the same substance. In this way God becomes apparent to us through nature, which in turn is an expression of God. Although Spinoza was excommunicated for this notion, we could easily find within it the conceptualization of an all-pervasive deity. In Deleuze's work, the idea of difference and its expression is portrayed in a similar way. The world is univocal in its expression of difference. This is described, famously, as a 'single voice' that 'raises the clamour of being' (DR: 35). Univocal substance continually expresses itself without relating to anything outside of or beyond it. In this way the world becomes different endlessly, rendering temporary the momentary congealing of the already given into stable categories. Unity therefore expresses difference. 'Being is said in a single and same sense of everything of which it is said', Deleuze writes, 'but that of which it is said differs: it is said of difference itself' (DR: 36).

One of the central concerns in Deleuze's ontology is how this pure, univocal difference comes to be expressed. It is this account of the manifestation of difference that allows him to overcome the potential problem that an ontology of difference and repetition would be an indeterminate flux of being. Deleuze's concept of difference is dialectical. This is not like the Hegelian dialectic which is structured by opposition and negation and which Deleuze describes as perverse (DR: 164). Instead, Deleuze formulates a dialectic through which difference is generated in the process of different/ciation and the relation of problems and Ideas. In order to understand this process we must first turn to how Deleuze theorizes the actual and the virtual which, following Bergson, he utilizes instead of the distinction between the possible and the real. This refusal is based on the limitation of the possible because when it is positioned opposite to the real it is conceptually identical with it, and lacks only reality. Deleuze figures the relationship between the possible and the real as one of resemblance and limitation. He represents it in this way because while the movement between the possible and the real is one of realization, it is the realization of what already exists in the possible and does not create anything new (DR: 211). The binary structure of possible/real excludes the possibility of the kind of difference that both Bergson and Deleuze value because it relies on pre-established possibilities and privileges identity. Moreover, this possible is projected backward after the real comes into being. Accordingly, Deleuze writes: 'it is not the real that resembles the possible, it is the possible that resembles the real, because it has been abstracted from the real once made, arbitrarily extracted from the real like a sterile double' (B: 98). The problem with the possible is that it depends on the real.

Bergson's alternative distinction to the possible/real is the virtual/ actual. For Deleuze both the actual and the virtual are real even if only the actual takes on a physical form. The separation of these concepts suggests a duality that is not altogether accurate because both are permanently imbricated in one another, caught in a process of constant interaction and mutual formation. Deleuze describes this as a circuit (D: 151). The virtual/actual structure is significant because it means that becoming does not move from actuality to actuality but is involved in a more complex relationship with the virtual. This is what enables the process of different/citation, which is part of the vitalism of Deleuze's work. 'Life', he writes, 'is the process of difference' (BCD: 50). The process of different/ciation is a complex system for describing the relationship between the virtual and the actual: differentiation is the reciprocally determining relation of ideas in the virtual, and differenciation is the movement by which the virtual idea becomes actual. This process takes place in the virtual, and comprises the differential relations of ideas, singularities and the problems posed that differentiate each other. Collectively they engender a response through the differenciation of actual things (DR: 207). The virtual realm of ideas is a differential space of differentiation in which problems emerge. Significantly, neither differentiation nor differenciation involves negation (DR: 207).

It is now clear why Deleuze preferred the virtual/actual to the possible/real structure, which consists of representation and consistency. Because the virtual does not resemble the actual, divergence is prioritized. The movement from virtual idea to actualized form is not one of identity because it is not a structure that incorporates the possible (DR: 191). The idea will therefore manifest itself in the actual along 'divergent lines' (DR: 212) as something novel. The movement of the virtual to the actual privileges difference and creation. In this way, Deleuze draws from Bergson a method of theorizing the dynamism of matter. Deleuze insists that if we examine only actualized things and ignore the process by which they come to have actuality then we see only differences in degree (B: 101), or how things differ from each other. We need to find ways to conceptualize a difference that is autonomous and expressed positively.

What Deleuze arrives at is a notion of difference that manifests not through external comparison or contradiction, but, rather, as an internal property of being. For Deleuze difference is creative, singular, genetic and differential; it does not emerge through pre-established structures because it already has the capacity to produce itself. Structure does not precede genesis but emerges as a way of organizing genetic and molecular differences. What Deleuze offers is fundamentally a differential ontology.[2] For Deleuze, the interaction of differences with one another engenders the production of further difference. Difference exists in a relational structure of reciprocal determination, presenting a system of manifestation in which the negative is afforded no constitutive power. Instead of a logic of opposition, negation and contradiction, Deleuze suggests that difference manifests through a reciprocal synthesis by which the differences internal to each component are expressed.

Deleuze is not interested in a static notion of being, instead he wants to develop an ontological understanding of what difference does. This is why he favours the dynamism of becoming over being, and the repetition of difference over that of the same. For Deleuze difference is fundamentally generative. Daniel Smith aptly summarizes Deleuze's ontology as 'Being = Difference = the New' (2007: 3). He distinguishes the idea of the new from such related concepts as change, causality or emergence because he understands that the Deleuzian 'new' operates at the most fundamental ontological level (2007: 3). Although difference is, for Deleuze, the condition of being, it manifests itself creatively as becoming. This radical notion of the new must be stripped of its positivist associations because it cannot be correlated with progress. Rather, the new is inevitable as it is when Deleuze theorizes the eternal return of difference through difference and repetition. In the next section I will examine what Deleuze's dynamic notion of difference means for how we think about political representation. This is one of the ways that the tension between structure and genesis plays out in Deleuze's work because politics is a frame for the incessant flux of wild and untamed difference that he offers us.

Identity and political representation

Deleuze's ontology of difference and repetition poses particular challenges for conceiving of feminist theory in relation to politics. Foremost amongst these is that his commitment to a philosophy of difference is also a critique of identity. The difficulty of this is that when we talk about politics we often assume that it involves particular identity groups struggling for representation.

Historically, the group that feminism has been understood to represent is 'women'. This becomes problematic in relation to Deleuze's work because for him identity cannot be a foundational category. Instead, it exists as a secondary and temporary effect of what is really going on: the endless proliferation of being as difference. This means that the world is first and foremost made up of differences but sometimes these differences sediment into patterns that create the effect of identity. We have to remember that when we look to the world and see around us identity, rather than difference, we should not make the mistake of imagining that these identities have metaphysical or essential status nor that they will remain unchanged through time. This means that a Deleuzian feminism cannot be an identity politics. While this rejection of identity creates difficulties for conceiving of political representation, it also opens feminism to difference in a variety of ways.

Questions of identity and difference have always troubled feminist theory. Through the first and second wave of feminism the concept of woman as a stable identity position was easier to defend. However, with the general valuing of difference in the poststructuralist feminism of the third wave any claim on an innate or essential identity for women became harder to sustain. These feminists debated the use-value of the category 'woman' for grounding feminist politics. If gender and sexuality are shown to be social constructions then there can be no uncontested 'woman' at the foundation of feminist politics, a problematic notion for a movement that has previously been based on common attributes and a shared identity. The questions that are imperative to this intersection is: what are the building blocks that feminism is left with from which it can construct a politics after the destabilization of the sexed subject? How can 'woman' be thought outside fixed and essential identities?

When third wave feminists asserted that sex, gender and sexuality are cultural constructs they remind us that the current organization of gender and sexuality within patriarchy, and the cultural meanings that are attributed to these categories, are not immutable. Moreover, to utilize an identity category to ground politics is based on a problematic system of inclusion and exclusion. The certainty of the category of 'woman' is always already contested because of the different ways that sex and gender can be defined: anatomically, chromosomally, by physical appearance or through self-identification. Butler cautions that when we utilize categories such as 'woman' we need to be attentive not only to how this category is constructed and unstable but also to how the category might be configured differently in the future. She writes: 'To deconstruct the subject of feminism is not, then, to censure its usage, but, on the contrary, to release the term into a future of multiple significations, to emancipate it from the maternal or racialist ontologies to which it has been restricted, and to give it play as a site where unanticipated meanings might come to bear' (1995: 50). This provides further reason to ask ourselves whether it is still salient to imagine that feminism is or should be *for* women. There is no doubt that historically it has been important for women to find autonomy from men in this political movement. However, it may be time to see feminism as a social project shared by everyone committed to challenging the problematic ways that patriarchy functions in our society.

Considering that Deleuze shares with third wave feminism the critique of unassailable identity categories, it should not be a surprise that it is in the third wave that his work is most fully mobilized for feminist projects. In fact, Deleuze's work provides us with a range of tools that could be useful for a dynamic feminist politics of difference. As such it would be a mistake to think that his work offers only a political quietism or a politics so abstract that it is out of touch with material reality. Rather, Deleuze's work pushes us to find political concepts that are adequate to his ontology of difference and repetition. A Deleuzian politics is therefore fundamentally about addressing reality, it's just that Deleuze's idea of reality is more complex than most.

Deleuze is talking about how difference works at a metaphysical level but we can utilize his ideas to tell us something about our material and political situation. In place of identity politics, Deleuze's work offers the scope for a politics of difference. This politics must concern itself with how we differ from each other rather than what we have in common and must address a world of differentiation, disparity, flux and becoming. In Todd May's book, *Reconsidering Difference*, he asserts the centrality and importance of difference as a political concept, claiming that most French thought after the Second World War is concerned with how difference should be configured and valorized (1997: 2). Although May is interested in the philosophy of difference, his arguments are framed historically through claims about the implications of philosophical systems in events such as the Holocaust, racism, religious fundamentalism and ethnic cleansing. Faced with these devastating annihilations of difference, he argues that 'the question of difference and of differences, of how to understand them and of how to respect them, needs to occupy us much more than it has' (1997: 9). But for Paul Patton this is not a question of validating any and all difference because difference can be co-opted for a discriminatory politics just as easily as for a progressive agenda, seeking to eradicate such discrimination (2000: 46). He writes:

> A politics of difference requires the conceptual determination of difference and the specification of relevant kinds of difference, in an ontological, ethical or political sense. This is how the French philosophers of difference have provided support for a politics of difference: not only by their refusal to treat difference as secondary, derivative or deficient in relation to a presumed identity, but also by providing conceptual grounds for the autonomy of individual differences and rejecting those forms of reductionism which treated particular differences, such as sex and race, as subordinate to one central difference or social contradiction. (2000: 46)

There are at least three significant reasons why Deleuze's philosophy is useful for a politics of difference. First, as Patton suggests, his conception of difference itself is imperative because, by locating difference at the foundation of being, he gives it a metaphysical status and reminds us that we will always have to account for how things are subject to change and metamorphosis. Secondly, by re-figuring difference in such a way that it cannot be subsumed by identity, he rejects binary configurations such as either/or, normative/deviant and us/them. Thirdly, the kind of difference he proposes is not based on current identities, but is instead abstract and differential. This is what makes a Deleuzian politics of difference open to the future. If we examine this matter in relation to gender (for example), it means that sexual difference need not be limited to an artificially binarized notion of male and female; instead, it enables a continuum of different sexual morphologies, not only as they exist in material reality but also as they may come to exist in the future.

Deleuze's politics of difference is, in part, a minor politics. In Chapter 2 I addressed the idea of the majoritarian and the minoritarian. I explained that the majoritarian is not a statistical notion (the category that contains the most people) but is a normative standard of measurement. In this case the majoritarian is composed of those who are afforded the most power and privilege in society: rational, white, heterosexual men. All becomings are becoming-minor which means that they enact a movement away from the majoritarian standard. Becomings are therefore molecular rather than molar; they do not consolidate established structures of power but undermine them.

Deleuze and Guattari's minor politics is committed to disrupting the established order. This politics is not concerned with including minorities within the body politic or what they call the 'majority system'. Rather, it is committed to the proliferation of minor becomings undermining structure and organization. They illustrate this through set theory, which is a method for studying collections of objects. Here the majority, which is denumerable and can be known, is contrasted with the minority, which is nondenumerable because it is in a process of becoming. The minority is engaged in forming unpredictable connections, enabling lines of flight away from the majority. They describe the minority as constituting '"fuzzy," nondenumerable, nonaxiomizable sets, in short, "masses," multiplicities of escape or flux' (ATP: 519). Within this configuration an axiom is a rule that holds up regardless of what it is applied to. The axiom is taken for granted as common sense and does not require explanation. The majority retains its place because of its monopoly on axioms, while the minority is what eludes them. In this way the power of the minority is,

> to bring to bear the force of nondenumerable sets, however small they may be, against the denumerable sets, even if they are infinite, reversed, or changed, even if they imply new axioms or, beyond that, a new axiomatic. The issue is not at all anarchy versus organization, nor even centralism versus decentralization, but a calculus or conception of the problems of nondenumerable sets, against the axiomatic of denumerable sets. Such a calculus may have its own compositions, organization, even centralizations; nevertheless, it proceeds not via the States or the axiomatic process but via a pure becoming of minorities. (ATP: 520)

The political importance of the minority is not in being included in or becoming the majority. The power of the minority is that it constantly unsettles the majority. Feminism is a minor politics when it struggles not for the recognition of women as an identity group claiming particular rights but when it undermines axioms that support patriarchy. This would not be the overthrow of patriarchy and the establishment of a new order but instead would unrelentingly undermine the hold that patriarchy has on power.

In *A Thousand Plateaus*, Deleuze and Guattari write of micropolitics and segmentarity. These concepts are also mobilized by Deleuze and Parnet in *Dialogues*, in their discussion of 'Many Politics'. Here they assert that politics needs not only to interrogate the lines of segmentarity operating at a level that is rigid and macro, but also at a more subtle and molecular level (D: 124). The social field is composed of both molar and molecular assemblages. At the molar level there are the binary machines dividing people into classes, sexes, ages, races and sectors (D: 128). At this level there is the molar woman, as distinct from the molar man. At the molecular level is a micropolitics, concerned not with structure and organization but with disruption, instability and dissonance. The figure of becoming-woman (the first stage of becoming through which everyone must pass) challenges the binary machines that organize the world in terms of man and woman. This is not, they write, a matter of adding another sex to the binary notion of sexual difference but of enacting a molecular sexuality, a line of flight that deterritorializes the configuration of man/woman (D: 131). The power of the line of flight is that it provides an escape route from established patterns and coherences. The line of flight is creative and experimental; it is not concerned with coding or overcoding but with mutation. This is not about the great ruptures in systems but 'the little crack, the imperceptible ruptures' which enable lines of flight to slip into gaps, everywhere (D: 131). Not only is this subversive, it is also militant and revolutionary: 'in fleeing to seek a weapon' (D: 136). This configuration of lines provides a distributed model of power. The molecular lines, the lines of flight, have the power to subvert molar organization. In this way everyday actions and experiments have the capacity to bring about change.

However, Deleuze and Guattari are not just advancing a minor politics or a micropolitics. There is always a tension in their work between the molar and the molecular when it comes to politics. We see this when they make an important comment about feminism and its relation to the identity category 'women' which, as we saw in Chapter 2, they describe as a molar entity. They write of the fight to be had at the level of the axiom, 'for the vote, for abortion, for jobs' (ATP: 520). This means that women do, on some level, need to conduct a molar politics when fighting for their organism, history or subjectivity. However, they caution: 'it is dangerous to confine oneself to such a subject, which does not function without drying up a spring or stopping a flow' (ATP: 304). The importance of this point cannot be underestimated. Deleuze and Guattari are not saying that there is no place for the kind of politics that addresses the macro structures of power or the identity positions with which we are familiar. In some ways this resonates with the strategic essentialism advanced by Gayatri Chakravorty Spivak in relation to postcolonial theory. Spivak (1996) suggests that there are instances in which it may be advantageous to appeal to a shared group identity to achieve concrete political ends. What she shares with Deleuze and Guattari is the idea that this appeal to identity is strategic and does not express an ontological condition. For Deleuze, politics needs to address molar organization but it cannot end there; it must always find space for molecular becomings.

Deleuze and Guattari compel us to undertake a macropolitics and a micropolitics at the same time (ATP: 235). The reason for this becomes clear when we look at the two types of multiplicity that they describe. The first is extensive; as a numerical multiplicity things can be added or subtracted without a change in kind. The other multiplicity is intensive and any change in its composition will be a fundamental change in its nature. This can also be thought of as the distinction between a quantitative and qualitative multiplicity. Changes at the molar level are related to the extensive multiplicity. A macropolitical change could, for example, mandate that women fill half of all political offices in government. However, this will remain a quantitative change unless the equal representation of women brings intensive change to the nature of political office (and of politics) itself. Moreover, this will do little to alter the way that sex and gender are understood in our society if women, in occupying these roles, adopt a male standard of measurement. Therefore, it is not enough to include more diversity in political life if all this does is include more people in existing structures and practices. Change to macro structures is important but only if it permits molecular politics and intensive multiplicities as well.

The tension between identity and difference that is central to Deleuze's work is also important to third wave feminism. It concerns how to address existing structures and identities while simultaneously undermining those systems and traditions that produced these structures and identities in the first place. Deleuze's work on difference reminds us of the teeming complexity of the pure difference that is present beneath any identity category. Because of this, we cannot give ontological status to a particular structure or identity when this is only a secondary manifestation of a much richer and more complex state of difference. However, identity is itself further complicated because there are many axes along which identity is organized and many identity positions that interpellate us as individuals.

Intersectional difference

When we look at the category of 'women' itself, we need to remember that this has never been coherent but has always contained within it a range of other identity positions. Braidotti acknowledges these differences in her notion of sexual difference, which operates at three levels: the differences between men and women, the differences amongst woman and the differences within each woman (2011: 151–7). These multiple levels at which difference operates further problematize difference in relation to feminism because it reminds us that identification is complicated by the way that any molar difference (such as the distinction between men and women) is always already riven by a range of other identity positions. These are not the molecular differences that undermine structures and identities but rather are the differences that offer us identity positions beyond sex. Throughout its history, feminist theory (and feminist politics more broadly) has been called to account for differences other than sex, such as those that emerge in relation to gender, race, class and disability. It is significant that some of these identity positions are overtly marked on the body while others may not be. Some of these markings are unchosen, such as skin colour, while others may emerge through specific and deliberate stylizations. But there is also a range of complex identity positions that may not manifest visually. This means that bodies can be organized in relation to their appearance or capacities, but also through complex systems of self-identification. However the result of any of these groupings of people is that individuals are subjected to a system in which they have a range of cultural intelligibilities and therefore cannot be reduced to a single political meaning.

One of the ways that the tension between difference and identity has been theorized is through intersectionality, which enables us to envisage the individual as located in relation to more than one identity position.[3] This framework developed out of the imperative to consider the relationship between sexual oppression and racial oppression, as well as the acknowledgement of how racial inequalities subsist within feminism itself. Jasbir Puar writes: 'intersectionality emerged from the struggles of second wave feminism as a crucial black feminist intervention challenging the hegemonic rubrics of race, class, and gender within predominantly white feminist frames' (2012: 51). As such, this approach to difference is attentive to how privilege works within feminism itself, and requires that feminism address a range of issues relevant to those outside the white middle class. However, intersectionality can be a problematic framework if it is used merely to silence those women who speak from a position of relative power or if it fractures feminist politics so much that a common objective cannot be found.

Intersectionality also risks becoming another, more complicated version of identity politics because it is interested in the locatedness of individuals within a matrix of different identity positions determined by factors such as sex, race and class. However, because these positions get inscribed with meaning *through* this relational structure we have to remember that they are not innate but are constructed through regimes of power. For example, an intersectional approach to thinking about difference has been fruitful for ecofeminists who have pointed out the structural relationship between the patriarchal oppression of women and the anthropocentric treatment of nonhuman nature as a resource for human exploitation.[4] This is because, as the animal studies scholar Richard Twine reminds us, an intersectional approach acknowledges the 'interdependencies between social categories of power' (2010: 398). Here, patriarchy and anthropocentrism are two different manifestations of a larger system of domination and exploitation. Acknowledgement of the way that power operates in complex and often invisible ways is important to feminism because power is exercised not only on bodies organized in terms of sex but also on a range of minority bodies including those that are non-white, non-heterosexual, nonhuman and disabled (as we saw in Chapter 4). This means that if intersectionality is an identity politics it is attentive to the contingencies of identity and, more importantly, it reminds us that it is imperative for feminism to engage with a more complex and multifaceted structure of oppression than just patriarchy.

The usefulness of intersectionality as a framework is contested in feminist work on Deleuze. Grosz, for example, is suspicious of intersectionality and writes that this involves already definable and distinct forms of oppression and constitutes a 'matrix of domination, a hierarchy of misery' (2011: 92). While distrust of the appeal to identity-based politics is important, it is undeniable that power is mobilized in relation to bodies that are grouped together due to their shared characteristics or capacities. Grosz here elides the potential for feminists to form productive alliances with other oppressed groups through a structural understanding of oppression. Rick Dolphijn and Iris van der Tuin are also critical of a representational notion of intersectionality (whereby different categories are linguistic constructions which are overcoded onto difference). They, like Grosz, are concerned with how the category 'woman' is always already besieged with other types of difference that remain irreducible to identity. However, for them a Deleuzian intersectionality could potentially eschew the understanding of difference in terms of identity categories and offer in its place a topological intersectionality, which measures the relatedness of things within a structure open to change. Within this framework difference is engaged in becoming and does not require comparison in order to exist. For them, intersectionality shows that beneath any category of oppression is 'a thousand tiny intersections' (2012: 140), which opens intersectionality to how things become other than what they were.

The benefit of this understanding of intersectionality is that it enables categories such as sex and race to become other while still acknowledging that things exist in relational structures, constructing alignments which are dynamic and fluid rather than secure. Puar also argues for the usefulness of intersectionality, in the service of which she mobilizes Deleuze and Guattari's notion of the assemblage. In her book *Terrorist Assemblages* she interrogates the way that gender, race, class, sexuality, nation and ethnicity are configured in relation to security, nationalism and responses to terrorism. Puar argues that the assemblage has the potential to make intersectionality more nuanced in relation to the complexities of difference. The figure of the assemblage allows difference to be proliferated through 'spatial, temporal, and corporeal convergences, implosions and rearrangements' (2007: 205), which frames intersectionality not only in relation to epistemology (the differences which are already known) but also ontology (how things will become different in ways that cannot be recognized by our systems of knowledge).

Feminist theory, even in its most egalitarian manifestations, has always had to negotiate ideas about difference. It must account for the differences between those grouped as men and those as women, but also the other identity positions to which individuals might feel political allegiance. Many of these identity positions emerge through relational structures of power and oppression. This means that feminism needs to be critical of patriarchy but also the other structures through which power is expressed. Deleuze is an excellent ally in this project. He offers both a macropolitics, through which we can think about established structures and identities, but also a micropolitics of molecular becomings and lines of flight. But, most importantly, Deleuze is the great thinker of difference. Instead of difference as contradiction and comparison he offers a notion of pure difference: an originary, proliferating difference that could never be contained within identity. Moreover, this difference is ontological which means that it subsists within being itself. A feminism committed to Deleuze's notion of difference is rich with its possibility. The vibrant complexity of difference renders identity categories permanently unstable and requires a dynamic politics. This is not a politics of representation but is attentive to the distinctions between particular bodies and the differential processes that engender further difference. The question is, then, not just of what difference feminism could be attentive to but also what newness feminism might bring into the world. In the next chapter I turn to the place of recognition in feminist politics and examine how Deleuze's work on difference as novelty poses a significant challenge to this framework.

CHAPTER SIX

Politics

Feminism is political because its concern is with what happens to power when sex, gender and sexuality come into play in social structures. What is meant by politics can shift in different disciplines. For example, political philosophy might concern itself with normative statements that express value judgements, in literary or cultural studies politics might be analysed through decoding how ideology subsists in representation and history might engage with politics through examining concrete structures and systems of governance. There are two things that are true of all of these different ways of approaching politics. The first is that politics is about how we imagine and enact collective life. The second is that politics is omnipresent; it is about how power and discourse move through every structure of relations between people in society.

As we saw in the previous chapter, Deleuze's work does not contain a clear political programme. This is exacerbated because of its abstraction, which can frustrate attempts to mobilize it to address our day-to-day political realities. Moreover, Deleuze's anti-humanism can make it difficult to locate a functional subject in his work. As discussed in Chapter 1, Deleuze displaces the bounded and coherent subject of Cartesian humanism through taking thought out of the subject and placing it in a world of differential problems. Although deeply suspicious of the subject as a transcendent entity, this is not to say that subjectivity is absent in Deleuze's work: he just did not want to confer on it a philosophical status that would elevate it above the immanence through which he imagines the world or position it as a timeless structure. This is because he regards the subject as the effect of micro and macro processes existing both beneath and above the level of the subject. His model of subjectivity is at odds with liberal individualism, the framework that usually grounds how we imagine the political citizen. This subject rejects those aspects of subjectivity that constitute how we imagine the political individual (such as agency, self-knowledge, consistency, coherence and the ability to effect change rather than be affected by it). As addressed in Chapter 5, Deleuze's work is not an identity politics. It therefore challenges conventional political discourse based on identity and the sovereign self. This chapter contends that despite this abstraction Deleuze's work is useful for feminist politics. Moreover, it suggests that it is precisely because it is complex, committed as it is to nonhuman thought, becomings, desiring-machines, bodies without organs and, most importantly, pure difference that it can address the world more adequately than a conventional politics of subjects, stable systems and identity categories.

This chapter articulates the possibility of Deleuzian feminism against a politics of 'recognition'. In political debates recognition has gained considerable currency because it offers a way for us to conceptualize the relationship between the subject and its surroundings, and as such it has provided a framework for theorizing the subject in community. Recognition, being premised on the intelligibility of particular types of subjects within structures of social meaning, has also been important for the articulation of identity politics. Because Deleuze's work offers a critique of recognition, it facilitates ways to think about politics and political community beyond the recognition paradigm. This chapter begins by examining what is at stake for politics in the recognition framework and how Deleuze might aid us in overcoming its limitations. It then further demonstrates the limitations of the recognition framework through comparing a Deleuzian feminism, exemplified by the work of Grosz, with the work of Butler who is both representative of political work on recognition and extremely influential in feminist political debates. Butler's work demonstrates what is problematic about recognition, namely, that it allows only a limited concept of alterity and grounds both subjectivity and intersubjectivity in negativity. Alternatively, Grosz argues for an affirmative and joyous feminist politics of 'imperceptibility' (2002: 470), which is open to the profound difference that Deleuze theorizes. The chapter concludes with the exuberant and experimental minor feminism, committed to imperceptibility rather than recognition, which we can construct from Deleuze's work.

Recognition and politics

The notion of recognition most commonly mobilized in politics debates has a Hegelian pedigree. As we saw in Chapter 5, Deleuze asserts his own concept of difference, in part, through a critique of Hegel. Both Deleuze and Hegel mobilize similar concepts such as difference, desire and negation. However, what Deleuze does with these concepts is fundamentally at odds with how Hegel uses them. It is because Deleuze is committed to challenging the dominance of Hegelian thought that he is *the* philosopher who can take feminism beyond the recognition framework and open it to the pure difference at the foundation of his own ontology.

For Hegel, recognition is a process through which the subject comes into being. It occurs through the ability to recognize the self as a subject, the conferring of recognition on others, and recognition or legitimation of the individual by the state. Therefore, it presumes a model of intersubjectivity, a structure which acknowledges a fundamental and constitutive relationally between individuals. Hegel's subject achieves recognition partly by finding itself reflected in the world and partly through being recognized by others. For Hegel the subject (and, in fact, all being) emerges through a dialectic structure, which is the mechanism by which he theorizes the transformation of being. Negativity is central to the dialectic because it describes a process through which things are constituted against what they are not (the negative). This is bound up with conventional understandings of desire because when formulated in terms of lack desire is framed as what is missing from, or external to, the self. Within this schema, identity comes into being through a relation to difference, which is conceived in terms of opposition. Negativity is not something that can be overcome but is carried within being as its constitutive condition. Ultimately this subject finds a reflection of itself by recognizing that the other is not only similarly struggling for self-consciousness but is also a desiring being. 'Self-consciousness', Hegel writes, 'exists in and for itself when, and by the fact that, it so exists for an other; that is, it exists only in being acknowledged' (1977: 111). The ultimate recognition for Hegel's subject is that in being constituted through this external negativity it is at one with the world. In his work this realization is described as the recognition of substance as subject. It is precisely because this subject comes into being through relationality that it has become an important figure in discussions of politics and to imaginings of community.

As Jean-Luc Nancy suggests, 'we read Hegel or we think him such as he has already been reread or rethought up to us, such as he has already been played out in thought' (2002: 7). The Hegel that we most commonly access, particularly in a French tradition, has been mediated through Alexandre Kojève's *Introduction to the Reading of Hegel* (1980), which has been influential in how Hegel is understood today. In Kojève's reading of Hegel the struggle for recognition is inherently violent and involves a 'fight to the death' (1980: 7). He emphasizes the place of desire in relation to recognition, writing:

> therefore, to desire the Desire of another is in the final analysis to desire that the value that I am or that I 'represent' be the value desired by the other: I want him to 'recognize' my value as his value. I want him to 'recognize' me as an autonomous value. In other words, all human, anthropogenetic Desire—the Desire that generates Self-Consciousness, the human reality—is, finally, a function of the desire for recognition. (1980: 7)

For Kojève, recognition is not about the realization of the harmony of subject and substance. Instead, the aim is to be recognized by others as a transforming being and one that acts upon the world.

The stakes are high in this debate for how political community is conceived.[1] As a political imperative, the fight for recognition is about asserting that a particular identity (or a particular type of subject) should be recognized by society and through this recognition comes legitimation. For example, feminists have long fought for recognition of women's status as full citizens. This is one of the ways that we can understand the struggle for the right to vote and property rights which once extended to women marked them as members of political and economic life. More recently we have seen the struggle for recognition in the gay marriage debate in which people have fought to have their relationship recognized by the state so as to legitimate their love and status as gay citizens. We also see this in the transgender, intersex and nonbinary rights movements through the fight to have a third gender recognized in legal documentation such as passports. Looking at these examples, it should not be surprising that recognition has been central to the identity politics associated with gender and sexuality, as well as those of race and class in the 1980s and 1990s. Recognition has been very important for thinking about how identity and difference function in society, and has proved useful for debates about multiculturalism and postcolonialism (Taylor 1994),[2] and also for feminism (Fraser 2003, 2005; Butler 1999, 2004, 2009). Nancy Fraser goes so far as to describe recognition as the 'chief grammar' through which feminism grounds its claims at the turn of the century (2005: 298). While the intention in turning to recognition is often to value difference, the risk is of complicity with regimes of visibility. In this way, recognition becomes coded as that which is visible and articulable and what is beyond recognition is rendered invisible.

However, the larger political issue with recognition is that demanding intelligibility can simultaneously erase difference and alterity. This is something that Derek Attridge alludes to in his work on the figure of the Other. He states that 'insofar as I apprehend the already existing other, it is not other: I recognize the familiar contours of a human being, which is to say I accommodate him or her to my existing schemata' (1999: 24). Moreover, recognition, with its reliance on what has gone before, supports established cultural values as if they were universal or innate. The politics of recognition has already been criticized by a range of theorists such as Grosz and Alain Badiou. 'In spite of its place in the rhetoric of radical politics since Hegel', Grosz writes, 'recognition is the force of conservatism, the tying of the new and the never-conceived to that which is already cognized' (2001: 103). The epistemological structure of thought categorizes and hierarchizes being so that it is reduced to systems that pre-date the particular encounter. Badiou, like Grosz, is deeply critical of recognition, particularly as it manifests in ethical theory: 'the whole ethical predication based upon recognition of the other should be purely and simply abandoned' (2001: 25).

For feminism, the problem with recognition as a social and political concept is that it covers over the complexity and plurality of difference. While many feminists, such as Butler and Fraser, assert that recognition is central to political being, we need to consider the ways in which this constrains alterity and to ask ourselves whether moving beyond recognition might enable feminism to grapple more fully with difference. This could facilitate a more nuanced appreciation of the differences that are central to understanding gender and sexuality but also those that fragment the individuals grouped under the category of 'woman'. The struggle is not, then, for the political representation of a certain identity but for rendering the category of 'woman' more open to difference. Abandoning recognition may appear, at first, to exude privilege. After all, there are many feminists who are still struggling to have their claim to fundamental human rights recognized. While I do not want to diminish this political struggle, feminist theory also needs to consider the cost involved at a conceptual level. The by-product of demanding the recognition of identity positions is that it contributes to consolidating macro categories like 'woman' and the 'human'. Moving beyond recognition and the fight for political representation as a group with a shared identity may in fact permit feminism much stranger and more vital encounters with alterity.

Deleuze's work is useful for critiquing the recognition framework because it offers a sustained and unrelenting critique of Hegel and his idea that difference is generated in relation to negation. As we saw in the previous chapter, pure difference is expressed without recourse to the negative. The version of Spinozist substance with which Deleuze works means that there can be no place for negation because, as Deleuze writes: 'negation is nothing, because absolutely nothing ever lacks anything' (S: 96). Moreover, in adopting Nietzsche's affirmation of difference through the eternal return, Deleuze commits to a version of difference that emerges through affirmation. 'Nietzsche's practical teaching,' he insists, 'is that difference is happy; that multiplicity, becoming and chance are adequate objects of joy by themselves and that only joy returns' (NP: 190). Deleuze finds in Nietzsche a world of competing forces that are not goal-oriented and are engaged in nothing more than their own expansion. This worldview makes Nietzsche's work a form of anti-humanism, which envisages the world in terms of shifting hierarchies and alignments, rather than in terms of subjects and objects. Stable entities, such as the subject, are only the momentary congealing of these forces.[3] Deleuze draws on Nietzsche's positive repetition to articulate a mode of difference beyond the reach of Hegel's dialectic. The eternal return enables difference in all its new and unrecognizable forms, and as such it is not engaged in repeating or consolidating identities. Deleuze writes,

> indeed, we fail to understand the eternal return if we make it a consequence or an application of identity. We fail to understand the eternal return if we do not oppose it to identity in a particular way. The eternal return is not the permanence of the same, the equilibrium state or the resting place of the identical. It is not the 'same' or the 'one' which comes back in the eternal return but return is itself the one which ought to belong to diversity and to that which differs. (NP: 46)

According to Deleuze, the recognizable is of little use to metaphysics. This is because difference is just too profound to be captured within a framework that privileges the recognition of what we already know.

Deleuze is also directly critical of the concept of recognition. In *Difference and Repetition* he asserts that recognition is instrumental in the concealment of pure difference. As we saw with the image of thought in Chapter 1, Deleuze is concerned that recognition is subservient to common sense. When we assume common sense, it generates a version of philosophy premised on the recognition of the familiar. '[R]ecognition', Deleuze writes, 'has never sanctioned anything but the recognizable and the recognized; form will never inspire anything but conformities' (DR: 134). Significantly, as with identity, Deleuze does not deny the existence of representation, or recognition, as they are experienced. In fact he suggests that recognition constitutes a significant part of our existence in the world. However, in his ontology of difference and repetition, in which identity manifests only after difference, recognition has but a minor place. Identity and the recognition that it enables are therefore secondary, and are nothing more than the derivative after-effects of the processes which give rise to difference as novelty. Moreover, recognition is banal and does not enable us to access the flux of pure difference that makes our world an exciting and terrifying place. What compels us to think, he maintains, is not recognition (which never perturbs thought) but encounters with what is strange and unfamiliar, or the 'imperceptible' (DR: 140). So recognition is not just limiting for how we think about the difference we encounter in the world, it also prevents us from engaging in thought.

A feminism that is neither an identity politics, nor centred on recognition can find significant resources in Deleuze's philosophy. This is because recognition determines that politics be articulated in relation to a structure that can accommodate only a limited version of difference, not the pure difference which we find in Deleuze's work. In the next section I contrast Butler's recognition-based feminism with Grosz's Deleuzian feminism of difference and imperceptibility.

Feminism beyond recognition

Butler's work has probably done more to shape current debates in feminist theory than any other feminist working today. This means that in critiquing the place of recognition in her work, we critique ideas that have become orthodoxies within feminist theory itself. In the preface to the re-released edition of *Subjects of Desire* in 1999, Butler defends Hegelian subjectivity, writing that the question to which she returns in her work is: '[w]hat is the relation between desire and recognition, and how is it that the constitution of the subject entails a radical and constitutive relation to alterity?' (1999: xiv). She cites the foundational place of negativity in her work as the justification for her rejection of Deleuze, describing his work as 'a manic defence against negativity' (2004: 198). Butler and Deleuze share a common interest in becoming, which they both position as central to ontology. However, Butler, taking her lead from Hegel, insists that this process is generated through negation, and that things are constituted in opposition to what they are not. For Deleuze, on the other hand, substance is self generating and becoming is the inevitable outcome of the eternal return of difference. The stakes in this differing treatment of the negative are high for these two thinkers. For Butler negation is central to the emergence of difference, while for Deleuze it is when negation is given a foundational role in ontology that the potential for difference is limited.

Butler's position on recognition is a powerful one and it is also deeply nuanced.[4] In adopting a structure of relation through the constitutive power of negation, Butler renders intersubjectivity as foundational and highlights our essential dependence on others.

In *Frames of War*, she describes this intersubjectivity as a binding to 'the subject I am not' (2009: 43), and she uses this to explain how difference is central to the formation of subjectivity. Because existence is confirmed by the 'acknowledging look of the Other', she writes, '[t]rue subjectivities come to flourish only in communities that provide for reciprocal recognition' (1999: 58). For Butler, recognition is also the regulatory matrix through which subjects come into being. Moreover, it is central to a politics of bodies: the body is a surface that exposes us to one another and it is a site where norms are policed and challenged.[5] Butler is particularly interested in the way that some bodies are recognized within our current configuration of gender and sexuality and others are not. Moreover, some bodies are recognized as human and others are not afforded the privilege that accompanies this category. She cites the dissonance with heteronormative bodies of those that are transgender and intersex. These bodies, she argues, are struggling but failing to achieve the status of recognition as human; they literally *matter* less within the 'norms that govern the appearance of "real" humanness' (2004: 28). Butler acknowledges the material effects of recognition, which contributes to shaping bodies in particular ways and also the (often violent) exclusion of those who are not recognizable in our current systems of meaning and value. Her project is therefore to expand recognition so that more diversity can be included in our structures of meaning and more people can be acknowledged as human.

In seeking an alternative to recognition as the dominant framework for feminist struggles, Grosz turns to Deleuze's work. Instead of negativity, Grosz's work is characterized by affirmation. She implores us, for example, to become more 'joyful in the kinds of struggle we choose to be called into' (1995: 6). This commitment to affirmation over negativity is a characteristic of Deleuzian feminism as we seen in Braidotti's work in which she asserts that feminism should remember the force of 'Dionysian laughter' (quoted in Butler and Braidotti, 1994: 41). For these feminists the rejection of negativity is not just a matter of tone: they eschew negativity as the motor of becoming, privileging instead Deleuze's notion of self-generating and proliferating difference. In this way they offer very different explanations of how the world manifests itself.

From the different notions of ontology that we see in Butler and Grosz's work come divergent ways of conceiving politics in general and feminism in particular. For Grosz, like Butler, feminism cannot be premised on a definitive notion of female and male subjects.[6] Here we see some distinct similarities in their objectives. While Butler (1995), as we have already seen, writes of rendering the category of 'woman' as a site of permanent political contest, Grosz insists that the task of feminism is to 'render more mobile, fluid, and transformable the means by which the female subject is produced and represented' (2005: 193). However, despite this common commitment, Butler and Grosz diverge in their realization of a feminist politics. Within her Hegelian framework, Butler's position is that we need to expand the 'grids of intelligibility' that govern recognition (2004: 35). So for Butler we live in relation to others and this lived sociality determines a structure of relation in which we are called to expand the framework of recognition in every encounter with difference. The notion of community in operation here is perpetually oriented to the future: we must always expend our epistemological frameworks so as to confer recognition on those who have previously been excluded. While her work on recognition is committed to expanding the gambit of legitimated identities, the Hegelian structure determines that things come into being in relation to pre-existing identities and norms. This does not mean that identities are fixed and conformity is the only option. Subversion is always a possibility for Butler's subject (1990) – gender, as we have seen, is an iterative practice and so there is scope to repeat gendered norms differently. However, even subversive repetitions are only possible in relation to a structure that pre-exists the subject. So although Butler is committed to articulating material differences these differences are always related to what has gone before. Grosz, on the other hand, discards recognition as part of a wholesale rejection of identity politics. For her feminism cannot be a politics of recognition. This would only further empower those who are socially dominant to confer and validate recognizable identities. Furthermore, it would require those who are not intelligible within existing categories to either conform or struggle to expand pre-existing regimes of meaning. This is why Grosz calls for a 'politics of imperceptibility' (2002: 470).

Grosz's politics is not a politics of coherent subjects but is concerned with forces beyond subjectivity. She suggests that if we understand subjectivity to be isolated and coherent we will fail to acknowledge the potentially infinite ways in which things can be interconnected, and in ways undetectable by models of identity (2005: 167). She writes:

> It is a useful fiction to imagine that we as subjects are masters or agents of these very forces that constitute us as subjects, but it is misleading, for it makes the struggle about *us*, about our identities and individualities rather than about the world; it directs us to questions about being rather than doing; it gives identity and subjectivity a centrality and agency that they may not deserve, for they do not produce themselves but are accomplishments or effects of forces before and outside of identity and subjectivity. (2005: 193–4, emphasis in original)

Theorizing these forces enables us to examine those things which both form and undermine subjectivity and which occur at scales both larger and smaller than the human. Grosz's feminism is significant because it dislodges the sovereign subject from the centre of analysis. Because this is a feminist politics predicated not on coherent subjectivities or identities but on the Nietzschean notion of mobile and competing forces, which renders the world perpetually in flux, the resultant feminism is a complex and multifaceted alignment of shifting forces. This leaves feminism with enough space to be contradictory and to represent many disparate interests and objectives. It would not be a matter, therefore, of replacing the current system (patriarchy) with something else. After all, Grosz argues, this would be predictable, and not particularly revolutionary (2000: 215). Grosz offers instead a version of feminism that is a process-politics characterized by incessant and endless struggle.

In *Becoming Undone* Grosz suggests that if the goal of feminism is conceptualized in terms of difference or equality then it has failed to deliver (2011: 75). Rather than looking to the history of feminism or to its current state, Grosz looks to the future in order to ask:

> To what can feminist theory aspire? What might it name, and produce? How can we produce knowledges, techniques, methods, practices that bring out the best in ourselves, that enable us to overcome ourselves, that open us up to the embrace of an unknown and open-ended future, that bring into existence

new kinds of beings, new kinds of subjects, and new relations to objects? (2011: 75)

Grosz here renders Deleuze's project of engendering thought and creating concepts as a central feminist concern. Concepts are multiplicities, which both constitute the world and herald the future. Grosz asks how thinking differently (about feminism, about sexual difference, about the world) enables us to engage in new social practices. Her call for a shift from the emphasis on the subject and epistemology to forces and ontology demonstrates the link between the corporeal feminism of the 1990s and the new materialism of today. This invites us to return to the body, contextualized within a world teeming with materiality. In this vein, Grosz insists that far from leading to political quietism, this politics, in relinquishing identity, would need to be committed to action (2002: 470). Moreover, this politics would prioritize the actions themselves rather than the people behind them. Such a politics is premised on contingent and shifting alignments of bodies and as such is open to future configurations of sex, gender and sexuality, subjectivity and the political landscape (2005: 193–4).

A Deleuzian feminism, as characterized by the work of Grosz, is not then about rendering political community in terms of harmony or inclusion. This is not an egalitarian feminism because it does not argue that women need to be recognized as the same as men. Nor is it an identity politics, which asserts the agenda of a particular group. Because of Deleuze's concept of an untamed difference any kind of recognition-based politics would only offer a poor approximation of ontological reality. Moreover, this could never be adequate to the richness of alterity and the profound shocks that experiencing this type of difference engenders. Difference is differential and encountering difference engenders further difference and produces a world abounding with diversity. Ontological difference is so wild that it constantly unsettles epistemology and our systems of sense. A Deleuzian feminism is a profound and joyous politics of difference and it has the space to be rich and complex by eschewing recognition. In the next section I consider what this politics of imperceptibility rather than recognition means for feminism.

A feminism of imperceptibility

To say that feminism needs to be committed to imperceptibility does not mean that this politics would be invisible. Refusing identity and recognition as the governing modes of feminism is not the same as making women or their issues disappear. Rather, it would be a feminism that troubles intelligibility. This is not, then, a feminism that demands inclusion within the regimes of sense promulgated by the current order. Instead, a feminism of imperceptibility is one that challenges the idea that sense is the only measurement of value. This feminism is fundamentally disruptive of current epistemologies and asserts instead the ontological: the endless flux of difference as novelty.

This politics could never be about disappearance because it is fundamentally a materialist feminism. It is committed to the acknowledgement of the material complexity of a world seething with difference, while at the same time precipitating the production of newness in the world. Therefore, this feminism is committed to the body both because it addresses the complexity of sexual difference and because it is constituted from actual material relations. This feminism asks: what can we make together? How can we find our desiring-machines? How, in bringing things together, can we produce more joyful affects? In being a politics of acts rather than identities, as Grosz suggests (2002: 470), a feminism of imperceptibility is committed to making things. Deleuze is invaluable for this project because he is fundamentally interested in examining what is going on at the molecular level of desire and in investigating the actual assemblages that come into being. This feminism would therefore be part of Deleuze and Guattari's larger schizoanalytic project. Instead of situating politics in the interiority of a sovereign subject, Deleuze grounds it in the spaces that connect all of us to one another and to the world we inhabit. To conceive of a politics that focuses only on these connective spaces involves a fundamental shift from thinking in terms of discrete subjects, with particular motivations and agency, to examining those spaces in-between discrete beings – the spaces where the action is taking place. This has the potential to make us less invested in personal struggle and commitments and more willing to find those connections and alliances that remake the world. Anti-identity positions are often criticized for leading to political relativism. However, in privileging becoming over being Deleuze offers us a politics in which actions are privileged over identities.

This is not, then, a politics of recognition that seeks better ways for women to arrive at intelligibility, better ways to articulate their issues or better forms of representation. It is not a feminism that asserts 'woman' as a foundation or grounding for action. The potential for this feminism can be found not in man or woman but in the *n* sexes that exist beneath these molar categories. The most important figure for this minor feminism is the becoming-woman: not an identity but a line of flight, a movement away from molar woman so as to open the pathway toward becoming-imperceptible. Exemplifying becoming-woman, the figure par excellence of this minor feminism is therefore the girl. We cannot be deceived by her small stature, or the cultural history in which girls have been framed as sweet, decorative, meek and obedient. The girl wields enormous power because she finds cracks and causes ruptures that bring systems of sense into crisis. A feminism of imperceptibility is concerned with those cracks and ruptures that unsettle and undermine the status quo. This feminism does not cover over incoherence but exploits it because these moments are problematic and generate thought. Deleuze is a thinker who has something to offer feminist debates, not because he proposes a theoretical answer that could operate as a 'catch all' for political dilemmas, but because he offers us something problematic and differential. This is not, then, just about bringing systems of sense into crisis but is also a creative endeavour; it generates new problems, new concepts and new ways of being. A politics of imperceptibility asks what new lines of flight might be possible, how these enable us to become more creative and how we might find new modes of political being.

One of the frameworks that a feminism of imperceptibility brings to crisis is liberal humanism. Articulated against this framework, feminism has been a struggle for inclusion within the pre-existing category of the human. As discussed in the first chapter of this book, liberal humanism assumes a universal standard: white, male, civilized, middle-class, educated, heterosexual, rational and able-bodied. For a long time feminism has fought to expand the category by asserting that women need to be recognized as subjects, as citizens and as fully human. Butler is also critical of the liberal humanist framework but the human is still the central figure in her work. In fact, the human is the avatar of her politics of recognition. While this figure of the human would be more accommodating and inclusive, in taking up the human and struggling for recognition Butler does not enact a sufficient break from the prior traditions that have afforded us this figure. A politics of imperceptibility enacts just such a break. It invites us to ask what it might mean to abandon this framework and the model of the autonomous and coherent masculine subject that it privileges. Braidotti has questioned why we would want to persist with Enlightenment man, writing: 'I have no nostalgia for that "Man", alleged measure of all things human, or for the forms of knowledge and self-representation he engineered. I welcome the multiple horizons that have opened up since the historical downfall of andro-centric and Eurocentric humanism' (2013: 195). If a politics of imperceptibility is premised on the rejection of the liberal humanist framework, there are two significant lines that we are invited to pursue: posthumanist feminism and nonhuman feminism.

Deleuze's work has, in part, paved the way for posthumanist thought. Posthumanism does not announce the death of the human or that it has been superseded. Rather it is premised on moving beyond the Enlightenment frameworks through which we understand the human. In many ways posthumanism is itself a feminist project because the same systems of thought that have elevated the human have also contributed to the oppression of women. As such, posthumanist thought invites us to question what it is that subsists in our systems of thought that has led us to the current state of affairs. We can see the value of critiquing these belief systems when we look at our own particularly tense moment in earth history: the Anthropocene, the geological age in which we see human impact shaping earth systems. We need to ask ourselves how the configuration of patriarchy, capitalism and anthropocentrism has led to the alignment of women with nature and the exploitation of both. How might moving beyond these frameworks enable a different existence for women and a different relation to the environment? A posthumanist feminism is premised both on the critique of the exclusions that inhere in and, in fact, constitute the liberal humanist subject and the simultaneous opening of this subject to the animal, to technology and to the inhuman. These can all be Deleuzian projects.

One of the ways that posthumanist feminism could manifest is as a nonhuman feminism. Liberal humanism places the human at the centre of its worldview; a nonhuman feminism decentres the human and reorients politics. Women have always been closer to the nonhuman than their male counterparts. A nonhuman feminism does not fight for the recognition of women as human but continues to move away from this category. Deleuze is the great thinker of the nonhuman. If we look at his work we see animals, objects, forces, systems and eruptions of nonhuman life. What is most significant about Deleuze's treatment of the nonhuman is that all of these entities and forces exist on a plane of immanence, affording them a fundamental ontological equality.[7] A nonhuman feminism moves beyond anthropocentrism, and would no longer be invested in human desires, interiority or systems. Instead of the interiority of human selves, this feminism would be oriented outward to the world. This reorientation would disrupt hierarchies that elevate the human above the less-than-human and would re-contextualize the human in a larger nonhuman world. This offers feminism a more-than-human scale on which to conceive of a feminist politics. This is a timely politics, as Colebrook reminds us. She writes: 'Feminism, today, facing the extinction of the human, should turn neither to man nor to woman: both of these figures remain human, all too human' (2014: 16). If feminism were no longer framed as a human prerogative, but as a force that has a life beyond the human, then it would be released from human thought and could have continued relevance after human extinction. This is the ultimate rebuke to post-feminism: a truly futural feminism. How exciting to wonder what this grand and devastating force of feminism could do to the terms of reference through which we understand life and politics itself.

A feminism of imperceptibility is therefore fundamentally oriented to the future. We see this because it is embodied by the figure of the girl, who, in not yet being a fully constituted adult, is rife with potentialities. Moreover, a feminism of the girl affords power to a figure that has never been fully human, both because she is female and because she is not an adult citizen. In rendering feminism fundamentally futural this is not to say that it is teleological. A Deleuzian feminist politics offers no final destination, and no definitive answers. There is no promise of utopia; that would be incommensurable with Deleuze's overall project because change is always unpredictable. This cannot be a feminism looking for answers because it is differential and problematic. In seeking out problems, feminism may find new approaches to the issues that face feminists today: the ways in which gender is represented and understood, the complex and often hidden ways in which power operates, and the risks associated with the post-feminist movement and the political complacency it invites. The pressing political issues that confront feminists today are largely permutations of the same issues that have faced women for a very long time. This includes political representation, gender and work, sexual violence, body image and sexual and reproductive freedoms. From Deleuze's philosophy a new generation of feminist theorists might find innovative ways to remain vigilant to these issues because his work offers a framework through which these old debates can be re-imagined and re-interrogated. However the most useful aspect of Deleuze's work is that it is a future-oriented philosophy. There are issues which feminism will need to confront in the future; some which do not yet exist and others which are not yet intelligible within our current systems of discourse. In opening us to this uncertain future, to the new eruptions of difference, to manifestations of sex, gender and sexuality that we cannot yet imagine, Deleuze's work is invaluable to a feminism which is not looking for orthodoxies but which can adapt to address new issues as they come into being.

NOTES

Chapter 1: Thought

1 For a feminist discussion of the mind's potential to exceed the body, which is situated in contrast to Grosz and Braidotti, see Eleanor Kaufman (2012).

2 This is evident in reports from Australia, the United Kingdom and the United States. For example, a 2008 report from Australia, which analyses data collected in 2006, suggests that while in the first year of a bachelor's degree there is actually a higher percentage of female students than male (between 2001–6 57 per cent of first year students were female) with this decreasing to relative parity by the final year (51 per cent female), this balance disappears as students progress through higher degrees with 39 per cent of students who start a PhD being female (Goddard 2008). The study also suggests that women hold 23 per cent of the (full-time equivalent) tenured positions in philosophy with few women in senior positions and a concentration in junior roles. This story is not unique to Australia. Statistics from studies in the United States and the United Kingdom have a similar narrative. A report from the United Kingdom written by Helen Beebee and Jenny Saul suggests that in their context 35 per cent of philosophy PhD students are female (compared to 61 per cent in English) and women hold 24 per cent of tenured positions in philosophy (2011: 6). An article by Molly Paxton, Carrie Figdor and Valerie Tiberius in the feminist philosophy journal *Hypatia* confirms that the situation in the United States is even worse. They cite the US National Center for Educational Statistics, which states that in 2000 women accounted for only 21 per cent of full-time faculty staff in philosophy programmes in American institutions (2012: 949).

3 These identity-based political critiques have fed into and augmented the denigration of the liberal humanist subject that has been enacted in postmodernism in which the stability, rationality and coherence of the subject have been called into question.

4   Deleuze also challenges Cartesianism through his privileging of Spinoza's monism, which enables a re-valuing of the body. This will be addressed in Chapter 4 when we come to consider Deleuze's work on the body

Chapter 2: Becoming

1   Deleuze elaborates on this example later in *A Thousand Plateaus* (324).
2   Pelagia Goulimari reads the claim that becoming-woman is a gateway to all other becomings as recognition of the success feminism has had in challenging patriarchy and facilitating women's desire to become other than the role allocated to them within this system (1999: 103).
3   See, for example, Grosz (2011) and Lorraine (1999).
4   On feminism and Foucault see, for example, Diamond and Quinby (1988), Butler (1990), McNay (1992) and Soper (1993). While feminists like Rosi Braidotti and Elizabeth Grosz were engaging with Deleuze's work in relation to feminism in the 1980s and 1990s, the first edited collection to consider Deleuze in relation to feminism, Ian Buchanan and Claire Colebrook's *Deleuze and Feminist Theory*, came out in 2000.
5   In an article on the place of Tournier's *Friday* in criticism of Deleuze from both Jardine (1984) and Peter Hallward (1997), Ronald Bogue suggests that Tournier was actually attempting to bring the problematic history of representations of capitalism and colonialism in the original text to the surface. He therefore reads the 'rape' of Speranza as a deliberate critique (2009: 129).
6   Braidotti finds greater feminist potential in Deleuze's work in later publications. See, for example, Braidotti (2001, 2006, 2011).
7   Animals in this *The Logic of Sense* are associated with depth, which is, Deleuze and Guattari write, 'no longer a compliment' (LS: 9).
8   Driscoll interrogates the ways in which feminine adolescence, or the literal ways in which a girl becomes a woman, intersect with the figure of the girl and the becoming-woman in Deleuze's work. For Driscoll, feminine adolescence is about the 'disjunctions and conjunctions between girls and women' (1997: 81). She highlights that, for Deleuze, Alice cannot become woman as a molar category (she cannot grow up) and maintain her capacity to embody the paradoxes that inhere in pure becoming (1997: 95). For Olkowski,

on the other hand, Alice's potential to grow up is more positive. She suggests that Carroll 'forgets to say that Alice will also understand the limits of language and logic, the limits of a limitless world of possibilities, a world without causality and identity, without the arrow of time, without signification or reference. And in understanding this, Alice will be not just a woman with a simple and pure heart but a woman who understands: a thinker ... a philosopher' (2008: 121).

Chapter 3: Desire

1 This is exemplified by the cultural myth that Queen Victoria did not believe that lesbians existed because sexuality was understood in terms of male desire for women (and even for other men).
2 See Bourg (2007) for a detailed discussion of intuitional psychotherapy and its impact on *Anti-Oedipus*. See Dosse (2011) for an account of daily life at La Borde.
3 Feminist criticism of psychoanalysis is diverse. The French feminists such as Irigaray, Cixous and Kristeva are often working in a psychoanalytic register but are interested in asserting a more positive place for women within this framework. For an alternative French critique of psychoanalysis in relation to feminism see, for example, Chapter 2, 'The Psychoanalytic Point of View' of de Beauvoir (2011).
4 For an extended discussion of Deleuze and Guattari's work in relation to the family see Laurie and Stark (2012).
5 Deleuze and Guattari engage with the desire for things that actually oppress us in relation to Wilhelm Reich (A-O: 29).
6 For a discussion of sexual publics see Berlant and Warner (1998). For a critique of the politics of intimacy in this piece see Laurie and Stark (2012).
7 See Lee Edelman's work on heterosexuality and futurity (2004).

Chapter 4: Bodies

1 For an important discussion of the differences between Anglo-American feminism and European feminism see Butler's interview with Braidotti (1994 and 2011: 86).

2   Deleuze's work on repetition in *Difference and Repetition* could also be mobilized to read the production of embodied identity in a similar way. First, the body can be thought of as something manifested in corporeal repetitions, active as well as passive. It can therefore never be correlated with the flesh of that Cartesian body which is merely the passive container of the active mind. Repetition, as Deleuze envisages it, gives the body the illusion of stability and identity, whereas in fact there are only corporeal habits. The claim is not that corporeal identities do not exist – for in fact they compose our material reality as we perceive it – but that they are a secondary sedimentation of other processes. Because the body is subject to corporeal stylization it cannot be considered a-historical. The body without organs exemplifies this process. There are always other ways to connect, and other things to connect with. This brings us to the second implication of Deleuze's elucidation of repetition, which is demonstrated by his third synthesis of time: namely, the movement to the future, which guarantees that things will become different through the eternal return. Bodies, therefore, cannot be thought of as static, self-identical or completed because they are always in the process of becoming.

3   While every body is subjected to the regulation of gender norms, this is not to say that these norms are inscribed on each body in the same way. We see this particularly in cases in which intersex bodies are subjected to medical intervention to make them conform to a model of binary sex.

4   Corporeal feminism is a branch of feminist theory that makes corporeality, and the existence of at least two types of bodies, central to politics. This movement includes Grosz's foundational text *Volatile Bodies: Toward a Corporeal Feminism* (1994), and also the work of a range of other Australian feminists including Moira Gatens (1996), Genevieve Lloyd (1984), Elspeth Probyn (1996), Zoe Sofoulis (1992) and Rosalyn Diprose (2002). The work of Rosi Braidotti can also be aligned with this movement. Not only does she have biographical connections to Australia but she also shares many of the commitments that characterize the disparate body of work of these thinkers. In her discussion of corporeal feminism as a specifically Australian movement, Patricia MacCormack asserts that these feminists all 'deal with French male philosophers, critically and sympathetically, with the body, and with queer sexuality' (2009: 85). See Grosz (1987, 1993, 1994).

5   Grosz's vitalist project can be correlated with a broader resurgence

of interest in life after the linguistic turn as characterized by biopolitics and new materialism.

6   See Grosz's discussion of the difference between Butler and Irigaray's deployment of sexual difference (2011: 107).

7   Grosz's discussion of non-normative families in *Becoming Undone* is somewhat problematic. In her discussion of how sexual difference is always in operation in attraction (whether heterosexual or not) she is critical of Butler's work on non-traditional families. She reads these families as a replication of heterosexual templates and describes the way that they 'express patriarchy as readily as the traditional family' (2011: 108) and frames them in Oedipal terms. In this way she ignores the many and varied ways that family is constituted and lived.

8   For Colebrook's discussion of Darwin in relation to extinction see her editor's introduction to *Extinction* (2012a).

9   See Shildrick (2002) for a further elaboration of this point.

10 Intellectual disability is particularly interesting because of its relationship with the Cartesian mind/body dichotomy. In this vein Hickey-Moody describes how people 'with intellectual disability are not imagined as incorporated, or material bodies that articulate a range of potentialities. Rather, their corporeality is assumed by default, as the difficult, fleshy packet that a deficient mind grew within' (2006: 190).

Chapter 5: Difference

1   For a discussion of the place of Hegel in Deleuze's work on the history of philosophy, particularly his work on Spinoza, Nietzsche and Bergson see Michael Hardt's *Gilles Deleuze: An Apprenticeship in Philosophy* (1993). See Deleuze's work in *Expressionism in Philosophy: Spinoza* (1992), *Spinoza: Practical Philosophy* (1988), *Nietzsche and Philosophy* (2006), *Bergsonism* (1991) and 'Bergson's Conception of Difference' (2000a).

2   For a more detailed discussion of Deleuze's differential ontology see Stark (2015).

3   Leslie McCall suggests that feminists have embraced intersectionality, which she defines as, 'the relationships among multiple dimensions and modalities of social relations and subject formations' (2005: 1771), more than other political groups and that

intersectionality is perhaps the most important contribution that women's studies has made to theory.
4   See, for example, Cudworth (2005).

Chapter 6: Politics

1   This way of conceptualizing recognition manifests in a more contemporary form in the work of Nancy Fraser (2003), Jean-Luc Nancy (2002), Axel Honneth (1996), Charles Taylor (1994), Judith Butler (1999) and Robert Williams (1997).
2   See Bignall (2010) for a useful critique of the place of recognition in theorizing postcolonialism.
3   There is a strong relationship between this conceptualization of a world of competing forces and the notion of a pre-personal flow of desire in *Anti-Oedipus*, which is expressed as pure positivity without lack. See Chapter 3.
4   See Stark (2014) for a detailed discussion of the place of recognition in Butler's work and specifically as a foundation for her ethical 'turn'.
5   In examining recognition in relation to embodied sociality Butler offers an important corrective to Hegel who, she acknowledges, positions the body as a mere container of consciousness (1997: 34).
6   Grosz explains that this is not the denial of sexual difference, but rather its 'increasing elaboration' (2005: 195).
7   For a further discussion of the nonhuman in Deleuze's work see Roffe and Stark (2015).

BIBLIOGRAPHY

Artaud, Antonin. 1976. *Selected Writings*. Edited by Susan Sontag. Translated by Helen Weaver. New York: Farrar, Straus and Giroux.
Attridge, Derek. 1999. 'Innovation, Literature, Ethics: Relating to the Other'. *PMLA* 114 (1): 20–31.
Badiou, Alain. 2001. *Ethics: An Essay on the Understanding of Evil*. Translated by Peter Hallward. London and New York: Verso.
Beauvoir, Simone de. 2011. *The Second Sex*. Translated by Constance Borde and Sheila Malovany-Chevallier. London: Vintage.
Beckman, Frida. 2011. 'What is Sex? An Introduction to the Sexual Philosophy of Deleuze and Guattari'. In *Deleuze and Sex*, edited by Frida Beckman, 1–29. Edinburgh: Edinburgh University Press.
Beebee, Helen and Jenny Saul. 2011. *Women in Philosophy in the UK: A Report by the British Philosophical Association and the Society for Women in Philosophy UK*. London: BPA/SWIPUK.
Berlant, Lauren. 2012. *Desire/Love*. Brooklyn, NY: Punctum.
Berlant, Lauren and Michael Warner. 1998. 'Sex in Public'. *Critical Inquiry* 24 (2): 547–66.
Bignall, Simone. 2010. *Postcolonial Agency: Critique and Constructivism*. Edinburgh: Edinburgh University Press.
Bogue, Ronald. 2009. 'Speranza, the Wandering Island'. *Deleuze Studies* 3 (1): 124–34.
Bourg, Julian. 2007. *From Revolution to Ethics: May 1968 and Contemporary French Thought*. Montreal: McGill-Queen's University Press.
Braidotti, Rosi. 1991. *Patterns of Dissonance: A Study of Women in Philosophy*. Translated by Elizabeth Guild. New York: Routledge.
Braidotti, Rosi. 2001. *Metamorphoses: Towards a Materialist Theory of Becoming*. Cambridge and Malden, MA: Polity.
Braidotti, Rosi. 2006. *Transpositions: On Nomadic Ethics*. Cambridge and Malden, MA: Polity.
Braidotti, Rosi. 2011. *Nomadic Subjects: Embodiment and Sexual Difference in Contemporary Feminist Theory*. 2nd edn. New York: Columbia University Press.

Braidotti, Rosi. 2013. *The Posthuman*. Cambridge and Malden, MA: Polity.
Brooks, Ann. 1997. *Postfeminisms: Feminism, Cultural Theory and Cultural Forms*. London and New York: Routledge.
Buchanan, Ian. 2008. *Deleuze and Guattari's* Anti-Oedipus: *A Reader's Guide*. London and New York: Continuum.
Buchanan, Ian and Claire Colebrook, eds. 2000. *Deleuze and Feminist Theory*. Edinburgh: Edinburgh University Press.
Butler, Judith. 1990. *Gender Trouble: Feminism and the Subversion of Identity*. New York: Routledge.
Butler, Judith. 1993. *Bodies That Matter: On the Discursive Limits of 'Sex'*. London and New York: Routledge.
Butler, Judith. 1995. 'Contingent Foundations: Feminism and the Question of "Postmodernism"'. In *Feminist Contentions: A Philosophical Exchange*, edited by Seyla Benhabib, Judith Butler, Druscilla Cornell and Nancy Fraser, 35–57. New York and London: Routledge.
Butler, Judith. 1997. *The Psychic Life of Power: Theories in Subjection*. Stanford, CT: Stanford University Press.
Butler, Judith. 1999. *Subjects of Desire: Hegelian Reflections in Twentieth-Century France*. New York: Columbia University Press.
Butler, Judith. 2004. *Undoing Gender*. New York and London: Routledge.
Butler, Judith. 2009. *Frames of War: When is Life Grievable?* London and New York: Verso.
Butler, Judith and Rosi Braidotti. 1994. 'Rosi Braidotti with Judith Butler: Feminism by Any Other Name'. *Differences: A Journal of Feminist Cultural Studies* 6 (2–3): 27–61.
Cixous, Hélène. 1976. 'The Laugh of the Medusa'. Translated by Keith Cohen and Paula Cohen. *Signs* 1 (4): 875–93.
Colebrook, Claire. 2012a. 'Introduction: Extinction. Framing the End of Species'. In *Extinction*, edited by Claire Colebrook. Ann Arbor, MI: Open Humanities Press. Available online: http://www.livingbooksaboutlife.org/books/Extinction (accessed 18 May 2016).
Colebrook, Claire. 2012b. 'Sexual Indifference'. In *Telemorphosis: Theory in the Era of Climate Change, Vol. 1*, edited by Tom Cohen, 167–82. Ann Arbor, MI: Open Humanities Press.
Colebrook, Claire (ed.). 2014. *Sex After Life: Essays on Extinction, Vol. 2*. Ann Arbor, MI: Open Humanities Press.
Cudworth, Erika. 2005. *Developing Ecofeminist Theory: The Complexity of Difference*. Basingstoke: Palgrave Macmillan.
Defoe, Daniel. 1868. Robinson Crusoe. London: Macmillan.
Deleuze, Gilles. 1988. *Spinoza: Practical Philosophy*. Translated by Robert Hurley. San Francisco: City Lights Books.

Deleuze, Gilles. 1990. *The Logic of Sense*. Translated by Mark Lester with Charles Stivale. New York: Columbia University Press.
Deleuze, Gilles. 1991. *Bergsonism*. Translated by Hugh Tomlinson and Barbara Habberjam. New York: Zone Books.
Deleuze, Gilles. 1992. *Expressionism in Philosophy: Spinoza*. Translated by Martin Joughin. New York: Zone Books.
Deleuze, Gilles. 1994. *Difference and Repetition*. Translated by Paul Patton. New York: Columbia University Press.
Deleuze, Gilles. 2000a. 'Bergson's Conception of Difference'. Translated by Melissa McMahon. In *The New Bergson*, edited by John Mullarky, 42–65. Manchester: Manchester University Press.
Deleuze, Gilles. 2000b. *Proust and Signs*. Translated by Richard Howard. Minneapolis: University of Minnesota Press.
Deleuze, Gilles. 2004. *Desert Islands and Other Texts 1953–1974*. Translated by Mike Taormina. London and Cambridge, MA: MIT Press.
Deleuze, Gilles. 2006. *Nietzsche and Philosophy*. Translated by Hugh Tomlinson. New York: Columbia University Press.
Deleuze, Gilles. 2007. *Two Regimes of Madness: Texts and Interviews 1975–1995*. Edited by David Lapoujade. Translated by Ames Hodges and Mike Taormina. New York and Los Angeles: Semiotext(e).
Deleuze, Gilles and Félix Guattari. 1986. *Kafka: Toward a Minor Literature*. Translated by Dana Polan. Minneapolis and London: University of Minnesota Press.
Deleuze, Gilles and Félix Guattari. 1994. *What is Philosophy?* Translated by Hugh Tomlinson and Graham Burchell. New York: Columbia University Press.
Deleuze, Gilles and Félix Guattari. 2004. *A Thousand Plateaus: Capitalism and Schizophrenia*. Translated by Brian Massumi. London: Continuum.
Deleuze, Gilles and Félix Guattari. 2005. *Anti-Oedipus: Capitalism and Schizophrenia*. Translated by Robert Hurley, Mark Seem and Helen R. Lane. Minneapolis: Minnesota University Press.
Deleuze, Gilles and Claire Parnet. 2002. *Dialogues*. Translated by Hugh Tomlinson and Barbara Habberjam. New York: Columbia University Press.
Derrida, Jacques. 1976. *Of Grammatology*. Translated by Gayatri Chakravorty Spivak. Baltimore, MD: Johns Hopkins University Press.
Diamond, Irene and Lee Quinby, eds. 1988. *Feminism and Foucault: Reflections on Resistance*. Boston: Northeastern University Press.
Diprose, Rosalyn. 2002. *Corporeal Generosity: On Giving with Nietzsche, Merleau-Ponty, and Levinas*. Albany: State University of New York Press.

Dolphijn, Rick and Iris van der Tuin. 2012. 'A Thousand Intersections: Linguisticism, Feminism, Racism and Deleuzian Becomings'. In *Deleuze and Race*, edited by Arun Saldanha and Jason Michael Adams, 129–43. Edinburgh: Edinburgh University Press.

Dosse, François. 2011. *Gilles Deleuze and Félix Guattari: Intersecting Lives*. Translated by Deborah Glassman. New York: Columbia University Press.

Driscoll, Catherine. 1997. 'The Little Girl: Deleuze and Guattari'. In *Critical Assessments of Leading Philosophers, Vol 3*, edited by Gary Genosko, 1462–79. London: Routledge.

Driscoll, Catherine. 2000. 'The Woman in Process: Deleuze, Kristeva and Feminism'. In *Deleuze and Feminist Theory*, edited by Ian Buchanan and Claire Colebrook, 64–85. Edinburgh: Edinburgh University Press.

Edelman, Lee. 2004. *No Future: Queer Theory and the Death Drive*. Durham, NC: Duke University Press.

Foucault, Michel. 1977. *Language, Counter-Memory, Practice: Selected Essays and Interviews*. Edited by Donald F. Bouchard. Translated by Donald F. Bouchard and Sherry Simon. Ithaca, NY: Cornell University Press.

Foucault, Michel. 1989a. *The Archaeology of Knowledge*. Translated by A. M. Sheridan Smith. London and New York: Routledge.

Foucault, Michel. 1989b. *The Order of Things: An Archaeology of the Human Sciences*. London and New York: Routledge.

Fraser, Nancy. 2003. 'Social Justices in the Age of Identity Politics: Redistribution, Recognition, and Participation'. In *Redistribution or Recognition?: A Political Philosophical Exchange*, edited by Nancy Fraser and Axel Honneth, 7–119. London and New York: Verso.

Fraser, Nancy. 2005. 'Mapping the Feminist Imagination: From Redistribution to Recognition to Representation'. *Constellations* 12 (3): 295–307.

Freud, Sigmund. 2001. 'Some Psychical Consequences of the Anatomical Distinction between the Sexes'. In *The Standard Edition of the Complete Psychological Works of Sigmund Freud, Vol 19: The Ego and the Id and Other Works*, translated by James Strachey with Anna Freud, Alix Strachey and Alan Tyson, 248–60. London: Vintage.

Freud, Sigmund. 2011. *Three Essays on the Theory of Sexuality*. Translated by James Strachey. Eastford, CT: Martino.

Friedan, Betty. 2010. The Feminine Mystique. New York: W. W. Norton.

Gatens, Moira. 1996. *Imaginary Bodies: Ethics, Power and Corporeality*. New York and London: Routledge.

Gatens, Moira. 2000. 'Feminism as a "Password": Re-thinking the

"Possible" with Spinoza and Deleuze'. *Hypatia: A Journal of Feminist Philosophy* 15 (2): 59-75.
Goddard, Eliza. 2008. *Improving the Participation of Women in the Philosophy Profession: Executive Summary May 2008*. Hobart: Australasian Association of Philosophy.
Goulimari, Palagia. 1999. 'A Minoritarian Feminism? Things to Do with Deleuze and Guattari'. *Hypatia: A Journal of Feminist Philosophy* 14 (2): 97-120.
Grosz, Elizabeth. 1987. 'Notes towards a Corporeal Feminism'. *Australian Feminist Studies* 2 (5): 1-16.
Grosz, Elizabeth. 1993. 'A Thousand Tiny Sexes: Feminism and Rhizomatics'. *Topoi* 12: 167-79.
Grosz, Elizabeth. 1994. *Volatile Bodies: Toward a Corporeal Feminism*. Bloomington: Indiana University Press.
Grosz, Elizabeth. 1995. *Space, Time, and Perversion: Essays on the Politics of Bodies*. New York and London: Routledge.
Grosz, Elizabeth. 2000. 'Deleuze's Bergson: Duration, the Virtual and a Politics of the Future'. In *Deleuze and Feminist Theory*, edited by Ian Buchanan and Claire Colebrook, 214-34. Edinburgh: Edinburgh University Press.
Grosz, Elizabeth. 2001. *Architecture from the Outside*. Cambridge, MA: MIT Press.
Grosz, Elizabeth. 2002. 'A Politics of Imperceptibility: A Response to "Anti-Racism, Multiculturalism and the Ethics of Identification"'. *Philosophy and Social Criticism* 28 (4): 463-72.
Grosz, Elizabeth. 2005. *Time Travels: Feminism, Nature, Power*. Crows Nest, NSW: Allen and Unwin.
Grosz, Elizabeth. 2011. *Becoming Undone: Darwinian Reflections on Life, Politics, and Art*. Durham, NC and London: Duke University Press.
Guattari, Félix. 2006. *The Anti-Oedipus Papers*. Edited by Stéphane Nadaud. Translated by Kélina Gotman. New York and Los Angeles: Semiotext(e).
Hallward, Peter. (1997). 'Deleuze and the "World without Others"'. *Philosophy Today* 41 (4): 530-44.
Hardt, Michael. 1993. *Gilles Deleuze: An Apprenticeship in Philosophy*. Minneapolis and London: University of Minnesota Press.
Hardt, Michael. 2012. *The Procedures of Love*. Kassel, Austria: Hatje Cantz.
Hegel, G. W. 1977. *Phenomenology of Spirit*. Oxford: Clarendon.
Hickey-Moody, Anna. 2006. 'Folding the Flesh into Thought.' *Angelaki: Journal of the Theoretical Humanities* 11 (1): 189-97.
Hickey-Moody, Anna. 2009. *Unimaginable Bodies: Intellectual Disability, Performance and Becomings*. Rotterdam: Sense.

Hickey-Moody, Anna. 2013. 'Deleuze's Children'. *Educational Philosophy and Theory* 45 (3): 272–86.
Honneth, Axel. 1996. *The Struggle for Recognition*. Cambridge, MA: MIT Press.
hooks, bell. 2014. *Ain't I a Woman: Black Women and Feminism*. New York and London: Routledge.
Irigaray, Luce. 1985 [1977]. *This Sex Which is not One*. Translated by Catherine Porter with Caroline Burke. Ithaca, NY: Cornell University Press.
Jardine, Alice. 1984. 'Women in Limbo: Deleuze and His Br(others)'. *Substance* 13 (3–4): 46–60.
Jardine, Alice. 1985. *Gynesis: Configurations of Women in Modernity*. Ithaca, NY and London: Cornell University Press.
Kaufman, Eleanor. 2012. 'Toward a Feminist Philosophy of the Mind'. In *Deleuze, the Dark Precursor: Dialectic, Structure, Being*, Ch. 2. Baltimore, MD: Johns Hopkins University Press.
Kojève, Alexandre. 1980. *Introduction to the Reading of Hegel*. New York and London: Basic Books.
Lacan, Jacques. 1977. 'The Mirror Stage as Formative of the Function of the I as Revealed in Psychoanalytic Experience'. In *Écrits: A Selection*, translated by Alan Sheridan, Ch. 1. London: Travistock.
Laurie, Timothy and Hannah Stark. 2012. 'Reconsidering Kinship: Beyond the Nuclear Family with Deleuze and Guattari'. *Cultural Studies Review* 18 (1): 19–39.
Lévi-Strauss, Claude. 1969. *The Elementary Structures of Kinship*. Boston: Beacon.
Lloyd, Genevieve. 2004. *The Man of Reason: 'Male' and 'Female' in Western Philosophy*. London: Routledge.
Lorde, Audre. 2007. *Sister Outsider: Essays and Speeches*. Berkeley, CA: Crossing Press.
Lorraine, Tamsin. 1999. *Irigaray and Deleuze: Experiments in Visceral Philosophy*. Ithaca, NY and London: Cornell University Press.
MacCormack, Patricia. 2009. 'Feminist Becomings: Hybrid Feminism and Haecceitic (Re)production'. *Australian Feminist Studies* 24 (59): 85–97.
May, Todd. 1997. *Reconsidering Difference: Nancy, Derrida, Levinas, and Deleuze*. Pennsylvania: Pennsylvania State University Press.
McCall, Leslie. 2005. 'The Complexity of Intersectionality'. *Signs* 30 (3): 1771–800.
McNay, Lois. 1992. *Foucault and Feminism: Power, Gender and the Self*. Cambridge: Polity.
McRobbie, Angela. 2004. 'Post-Feminism and Popular-Culture.' *Feminist Media Studies* 4(3): 255–64.

Nancy, Jean-Luc. 2002. *Hegel: The Restlessness of the Negative*. Translated by Jason Smith and Steven Miller. Minneapolis: University of Minnesota Press.

Olkowski, Dorothea. 2008. 'After Alice: Alice and the Dry Tail'. *Deleuze Studies* 2 (Supplement): 107–22.

Pateman, Carole. 1988. *The Sexual Contract*. Cambridge: Polity.

Patton, Paul. 2000. *Deleuze and the Political*. London and New York: Routledge.

Paxton, Molly, Carrie Figdor and Valerie Tiberius. 2012. 'Quantifying the Gender Gap: An Empirical Study of the Underrepresentation of Women in Philosophy'. *Hypatia: A Journal of Feminist Philosophy* 27 (4): 949–57.

Probyn, Elspeth. 1996. *Outside Belongings*. New York and London: Routledge.

Puar, Jasbir. 2007. *Terrorist Assemblages: Homonationalism in Queer Times*. Durham, NC and London: Duke University Press.

Puar, Jasbir. 2012. 'I Would Rather be a Cyborg than a Goddess: Becoming Intersectional in Assemblage Theory'. *philoSOPHIA* 2 (1): 49–66.

Roffe, Jon and Hannah Stark. 2015. 'Introduction: Deleuze and the Non/Human'. In *Deleuze and the Non/Human*, edited by Jon Roffe and Hannah Stark, 1–16. Basingstoke and New York: Palgrave Macmillan.

Shildrick, Margrit. 2002. *Embodying the Monster: Encounters with the Vulnerable Self*. London: Sage.

Shildrick, Margrit. 2004. 'Queering Performativity: Disability After Deleuze'. *Scan: Journal of Media and Culture*. Available online: http://scan.net.au/scan/journal/display.php?journal_id=36 (accessed 20 January 2015).

Shildrick, Margrit. 2013. 'Sexual Citizenship, Governance and Disability: From Foucault to Deleuze'. In *Beyond Citizenship?: Feminism and the Transformation of Belonging*, edited by Sasha Roseneil, 138–59. Basingstoke and New York: Palgrave Macmillan.

Sofoulis, Zoe. 1992. 'Virtual Corporeality: A Feminist Perspective'. *Australian Feminist Studies* 15: 11–24.

Soper, Kate. 1993. *Up Against Foucault: Explorations of Some Tensions between Foucault and Feminism*. London and New York: Routledge.

Spivak, Gayatri Chakravorty. 1996. 'Subaltern Studies: Deconstructing Historiography'. In *The Spivak Reader: Selected Works of Gayatri Chakravorty Spivak*, edited by Donna Landry and Gerald Maclean, Ch. 8. New York and London: Routledge.

Stark, Hannah. 2014. 'Judith Butler's Post-Hegelian Ethics and the Problem with Recognition'. *Feminist Theory* 15 (1): 89–100.

Stark, Hannah. 2015. 'Discord, Monstrosity and Violence: Deleuze's Differential Ontology and its Consequences for Ethics'. *Angelaki: Journal of the Theoretical Humanities* 20 (4): 211–24.

Taylor, Charles. 1994. 'The Politics of Recognition'. In *Multiculturalism: Examining the Politics of Recognition*, edited by Amy Gutmann, 25–74. Princeton, NJ: Princeton University Press.

Tournier, Michel. 1997 [1967/69]. *Friday*. Translated by Norman Denny. Baltimore, MD: Johns Hopkins University Press.

Twine, Richard. 2010. 'Intersectional Disgust? Animals and (Eco) Feminism'. *Feminism and Psychology* 20 (3): 397–406.

Williams, Robert R. 1997. *Hegel's Ethics of Recognition*. Berkeley, Los Angeles and London: University of California Press.

Winterson, Jeanette. 2011. *Why Be Happy When You Could Be Normal?* London: Jonathan Cape.

Wollstonecraft, Mary. 2004. *A Vindication of the Rights of Woman*. London: Penguin.

Woolf, Virginia. 1977 [1929]. *A Room of One's Own*. London, Glasgow, Toronto, Sydney and Auckland: Grafton.

INDEX

Ain't I a Woman (hooks) 15
Algeria 43
Alice (in Wonderland) 34–5
animal studies 11–12, 94
anthropocentrism 11–12, 37, 94–5, 113, 114
Anti-Oedipus (Deleuze, Guattari) 4, 41, 42–5, 47, 48, 49, 52, 53, 54, 57, 67, 68
anti-psychiatry 43–4, 45
   La Borde *see* La Borde (psychiatric hospital)
Archaeology of Knowledge, The (Foucault) 42
Aristotle 80, 81
Artaud, Antonin 74
   To Have Done with the Judgement of God 74
assemblage 91, 96, 111
   bodies, and 71, 74, 77
   desire, and 49, 52, 58
   Terrorist Assemblages (Puar) 96
   wasp/orchid nuptials 25
Attridge, Derek 103

Badiou, Alain 103
Beauvoir, Simone de 9–10, 16, 63
   The Second Sex 9–10, 16, 63
becoming 3–4, 25–40, 52, 54, 71, 73, 77, 85
   becoming-woman *see* becoming-woman

   being, and 86, 112
   feminism and the future 4, 37–40, 114
   molecular becomings 35, 80, 96
   the girl 4, 26, 33, 34–7, 40, 46, 112, 114
   wasp/orchid nuptials 25
becoming-animal 25, 26, 28, 34, 37
becoming-cellular 26
becoming-child 26, 28, 34, 37
becoming-elementary 26
becoming-imperceptible 3, 25, 26, 28, 36–7, 112
becoming-intense 25
becoming-minor 3, 4, 28, 36, 37, 90
becoming-molar 27
becoming-molecular 26, 27
Becoming Undone (Grosz) 68, 109
becoming-vegetable 26
becoming-woman 3–4, 23, 26–34, 36–7, 40, 91, 112
   molar/molecular disparity 26–8, 29, 35, 36, 37, 40
Bergson (Henri) 81, 84, 85
Berlant, Lauren 57
   Desire/Love 57
bodies 4–5, 22, 61–78, 94, 95, 96, 100, 107, 110
   body politic 65, 73, 77, 90

body without organs 29, 52, 62, 74–6, 77, 100
Cartesian devaluing of 3, 7, 8, 10, 18, 30, 59, 61–2
disabled *see* disability/disabled bodies
erotic *see* eroticism
materiality of 63, 65, 66, 110
minority bodies 95 *see also* disability/disabled bodies; race
non-normative *see* disability/disabled bodies
power, and 64, 65, 71, 72, 74
queer 64, 76
re-valuing of 3, 5, 66, 118
sex and gender 63–6
sexual difference *see* sexual difference
Spinoza 70–1, 72, 74, 75, 76, 77
Western philosophy, in 61–2, 65, 76, 78
what can bodies do? 70–8
women, of *see* women's bodies
Bodies that Matter (Butler) 64
Bogue, Ronald 32
Braidotti, Rosi 3, 7, 26, 29, 32–3, 66, 93, 107, 113
Patterns of Dissonance 8, 32
Brooks, Ann 38–9
Buchanan, Ian 42–3
Butler, Judith 6, 16, 64–5, 68, 88, 100, 103, 106–8, 112–13
Bodies that Matter 64
Frames of War 107
recognition, concept of 100, 103, 106–8, 112–13
Subjects of Desire 106

capitalism
desire, restrictions on 41, 47–8, 49, 50, 51, 55
nuclear family, and 47–8, 50, 67, 68
schizophrenia, relation to 41, 50–1, 74
Capitalism and Schizophrenia (Deleuze, Guattari) 41, 74
Carroll, Lewis 34, 35
Cartesianism 15, 19, 20, 22, 61, 64, 65, 99
Cartesian *cogito* 18–19
devaluing of the body 3, 7, 8, 10, 18, 22, 30, 59, 61–2
mind/body dualism 7, 61–2, 64, 65–6, 77, 99
castration complex (Freud) 46, 47, 54, 56, 58
children 33, 34, 35, 47, 62, 67
becoming-child 26, 28, 34, 37
Cixous, Hélène 16–17, 33
'The Laugh of the Medusa' 16
class 11, 15, 16, 17, 27, 40, 68, 91, 103
intersectionality, and 93, 94, 96
middle-class 11, 15, 39, 94, 112
working-class 15
Colebrook, Claire 40, 66, 69–70, 114
colonialism 11, 31
see also postcolonialism
Cooper, David 45
corporeal feminism 64, 65, 110
creative destruction 1, 3
Cressole, Michel 48
culture/nature binary 64, 65, 66

Defoe (Daniel) 30
Robinson Crusoe 30–2
Derrida, Jacques 32, 42
Of Grammatology 42
Descartes, René *see* Cartesianism
desire 16, 22, 29, 30, 31, 40, 41–59, 102, 106

INDEX

assemblage, and 52, 58
  eroticism 4, 42, 54–9
  Freud, and 45–6, 48, 49, 50
  Hegel (G.W.) 45
  La Borde *see* La Borde (psychiatric hospital)
  psychoanalysis, and 4, 40, 41–9, 50, 53, 56, 57–8
  sexuality, and 4, 33, 40, 41, 45, 50, 54, 55, 56, 57, 58, 68
Subjects of Desire (Butler) 106
Desire/Love (Berlant) 57
desiring-machines 4, 29, 41, 49–53, 54–5, 56, 57, 58, 100, 111
Dialogues (Deleuze, Parnet) 28, 91
difference 5–6, 79–97, 110
  concept of 79–80, 89, 101, 110
  eternal return, and 82–3, 86, 104–5, 106
  identity, and 78, 79–80, 81, 82–3, 84, 85, 93–4
  intersectional difference 6, 80, 93–7
  politics of *see* identity politics
  possible/real binary 84–5
  pure difference 79, 80–6, 93, 96, 100, 101, 104, 105, 106
  Reconsidering Difference (May) 88
  sameness/difference dichotomy 77, 83, 86
  sexual *see* sexual difference
  virtual/actual binary 84–5
Difference and Repetition (Deleuze) 1, 5, 18–19, 20–1, 42, 43, 79–86, 105
  'The Image of Thought' 20–1
differe*nt*/*c*itation process 85

disability/disabled bodies 5, 11, 59, 63, 76–8, 95
  intersectionality, and 93, 95
Dolphijn, Rick 95
Dosse, François 44
Driscoll, Catherine 33, 34

ecocriticism 11
ego 46, 53
Enlightenment 1, 3, 7, 17, 46, 113
  legacies 8–12
epistemology 17, 22–3, 96, 110
eroticism 4, 42, 54–9
essentialism, 4, 12, 15–16, 37–8, 40, 61, 80, 92
eternal return 82–3, 86, 104–5, 106
ethnicity 27, 96
  ethnic cleansing 89
  see also race

familialism 35
family 14, 37, 45, 46, 50, 55, 68, 73
  nuclear 41, 47–8, 67
  Oedipal *see* Oedipus complex
Feminine Mystique, The (Friedan) 14–15
feminine writing 16–17
feminism
  Anglo-American 5, 13, 16, 39, 62, 80
  beyond recognition 6, 106–15
  corporeal feminism 64, 65, 110
  Deleuzian 26, 38, 87, 100, 106, 107, 110, 114–15
  ecofeminism 94
  European 13, 16, 39, 62
  first wave 13–14
  French 16–17, 61
  futural 4, 37–40, 114

girl-power 38–9
identity politics, and 6, 80, 86–93, 94, 95, 96, 100, 103, 106, 108, 110
imperceptibility, and 6, 28, 100, 106, 110, 111–15
lesbian 15
liberal humanism, and 7–8, 12–17, 37, 112–13, 114
middle-class 39
minor politics, as 90–1, 92, 96
Muslim countries, in 13
nonhuman 113, 114
postcolonialism 15
post-feminism 4, 38–9, 40, 114, 115
posthumanism 113–14
riot grrrl movement 38
second wave 14–15, 87, 94
sisterhood 15
third wave 16, 38, 80, 87–8, 93
women of colour, and 15, 94
Women's Liberation Movement 15, 56, 58, 87
working-class 15
first wave feminism 13–14
Foucault, Michel 1, 29, 48, 50, 64
Archaeology of Knowledge, The 42
Order of Things, The 42
Frames of War (Butler) 107
Fraser, Nancy 103
Freudian school 43
Freud (Sigmund) 43, 53
castration complex 46, 47, 54, 56, 58
desire, and 45–6, 48, 49, 50
Three Essays on the Theory of Sexuality 46
see also Oedipus complex
Friday (Tournier) 30–2

Friedan, Betty 14
Feminine Mystique, The 14–15
functionalism 35

Gatens, Moira 61, 65–6, 73
gay liberation 58
gay marriage 102
gender 1, 2, 9, 11, 12, 16, 18, 30, 32, 38, 41, 67, 70, 89
equality 39
intersectionality, and 93, 94, 96
neutrality 12, 33, 61
politics, and 40, 99, 103, 107, 108, 110, 115, 194
sex, and 5, 16, 40, 61, 62, 63–6, 68, 87–8, 92
third gender 102
genderqueer see queer bodies
girl, the 4, 26, 33, 34–7, 40, 46, 112, 114
girl-power 38–9
Grosz, Elizabeth 6, 36, 65, 66, 68–9, 70, 95
Becoming Undone 68, 109
recognition, critique of 100, 103, 106, 107–10, 111
sexual difference 68–70
Volatile Bodies 36
Gynesis: Configurations of Woman in Modernity (Jardine) 29, 32

Hardt, Michael 55
Hegel, G.W.
desire 45
difference, concept of 80–1, 83, 84, 101, 104
Introduction to the Reading of Hegel (Kojève) 102
recognition, and 6, 101–2, 103, 104, 106, 107, 108
heteronormativity 2, 4, 54, 107

heterosexuality 11, 14, 15, 16, 45, 46, 47, 58, 64, 90, 112
    intercourse 56–7, 69, 70
Hickey-Moody, Anna 33, 77
homosexuality 69 *see also* gay liberation
hooks, bell 15
    Ain't I a Woman 15
human/nature dichotomy 52

identity 5–6, 11, 19, 37, 53, 54, 56, 57, 58, 78, 94
    becoming, and 25, 26, 34, 35, 37
    bodies, and 63, 70, 72, 73
    difference, and 78, 79–80, 81, 82–3, 84, 85, 93–4
    politics, and *see* identity politics
    see also class; disability/disabled bodies; gender; race; sexual preference
identity politics 6, 78, 80, 86–93, 94, 95, 96, 100, 103, 106, 108, 110
immanence 36, 50, 62, 75, 81, 99, 114
    thought, and 10, 20, 22
imperceptibility, politics of 6, 28, 100, 106, 110, 111–15
incest 31, 67 *see also* Oedipus complex
inside/outside dichotomy 52
intersectionality 6, 80, 93–7
    class, and 93, 94, 96
    difference, and 6, 80, 93–7
    disability/disabled bodies, and 93, 95
    gender, and 93, 94, 96
    race, and 93, 94, 95, 96
intersex 64, 102, 107
Introduction to the Reading of Hegel (Kojève) 102

Irigaray, Luce 3, 16, 17, 26, 29, 33, 68
    This Sex Which is Not One 29

Jardine, Alice 3, 26, 29–30, 31–2, 33
    Gynesis: Configurations of Woman in Modernity 29, 32

Kafka: Toward a Minor Literature (Deleuze, Guattari) 27
kinship 67
kin-work 37–8
Klein, Melanie 34
knowledge 3, 8, 21, 22, 71, 96, 113
    self-knowledge 19, 100
    Archaeology of Knowledge, The (Foucault) 42
    see also epistemology
Kojève, Alexandre 102
Kristeva, Julia 16, 33

La Borde (psychiatric hospital) 43–5, 50, 58
    liberation of desire 45, 58
Lacan, Jacques 32, 43, 46–7, 48, 56
lack/wholeness dichotomy 77
'Laugh of the Medusa, The' (Cixous) 16
Lawrence, D.H. 28
learning 9, 20–2
l'écriture féminine 16–17
Leibniz (Gottfried) 80–1
lesbianism 15
    see also gay liberation
Lévi-Strauss, Claude 67
liberal humanism 3, 10–12, 19, 22, 72–3, 76, 77, 78
    feminism, and 7–8, 12–17, 32, 37, 112–13, 114

literature 32, 51
  Kafka: Toward a Minor Literature (Deleuze, Guattari) 27
  minor literature 27
Lloyd, Genevieve 9
  Man of Reason, The 9
Logic of Sense, The (Deleuze) 1, 30, 31, 34–5, 42, 43, 74
Lorde, Audre 2, 15

MacCormack, Patricia 39
macro/micro political change 92–3, 96
majoritarian/minoritarian 26, 27–8, 29, 37, 95
  minor literature 27
  minor politics 90–1, 92, 96
  see also molar/molecular disparity
male privilege *see* patriarchy
Man of Reason, The (Lloyd) 9
marginalization of women 15, 62, 76
  Western philosophy, in 2, 3, 8, 9, 22, 33
  see also patriarchy
marriage 14, 67
  gay marriage 102
Marxism 47, 53, 54
materiality 64–5
  body, of the 63, 65, 66, 110
  culture, and 63
  sexual difference, of 62, 69, 70, 89
May, Todd 88–9
  Reconsidering Difference 88
May 1968 (Paris) 42–3, 45
McRobbie, Angela 39
mechanism/vitalism dichotomy 52
Miller, Henry 28
mind/body dichotomy *see* Cartesianism

minoritarian *see* majoritarian/minoritarian
molar/molecular disparity 6, 50, 52, 54, 90–2, 93, 112
  becoming-woman 26–8, 29, 35, 36–7, 40
  see also majoritarian/minoritarian
morphology 56, 61, 77
  sexual 64, 68, 89

Nancy, Jean-Luc 102
natural/sexual selection 68, 69
Nietzsche and Philosophy (Deleuze) 82
Nietzsche (Friedrich) 81, 82, 83, 104, 109
nonhuman feminism 113, 114
nonhuman sex 54, 56, 57, 58

Oedipus complex 4, 5, 31, 34, 40, 45–9, 50, 51, 53, 67, 68
  see also Anti-Oedipus (Deleuze, Guattari); Freud (Sigmund); psychiatry; psychoanalysis
Oedipus Rex (Sophocles) 45
Of Grammatology (Derrida) 42
Olkowski, Dorothea 35
oppression 6, 11, 12, 37
  racial 11, 94
  sexual 94
  structural nature of 6, 94, 95
  women, of *see* patriarchy
  zoomorphism, and 12
Order of Things, The (Foucault) 42
'otherwise Other' 31
Oury, Jean 43, 45

Parnet, Claire 28, 49, 91
  Dialogues (with Deleuze) 28, 91

Pateman, Carole 14
Sexual Contract, The 14
patriarchy 2, 4, 8, 9, 13–14, 17, 29, 39, 45, 46, 54, 87, 88, 109
   oppression of women 2, 12, 14–15, 32–3, 37, 91, 94–5, 96, 113
   phallus, power of 46, 56, 74
Patterns of Dissonance (Braidotti) 8, 32
Patton, Paul 89
Plato 20, 45, 80, 81
pleasure 4, 16, 17, 46, 50, 54, 69
   phallocentric nature of 54
politics 50, 78, 99–115
   body politic 65, 73, 77, 90
   gender, and 40, 99, 103, 107, 108, 110, 115, 194
   identity, and 6, 80, 86–93, 94, 95, 96, 100, 103, 106, 108, 110
   imperceptibility, of 6, 28, 100, 106, 110, 111–15
   macro/micro political change 92–3, 96
   majoritarian/minoritarian 26, 27–8, 29, 37, 90–1, 95
   minor politics 90–1, 92, 96
   recognition, and 6, 18, 91, 97, 100, 101–6
possible/real binary 84–5
postcolonialism 39, 92, 103
   feminism 15
post-feminism 4, 38–9, 40, 114, 115
posthumanism 11, 40
   feminism 113–14
   thought 113
post-modernism 39
poststructuralism 39
   feminism *see* third wave feminism
   thought 32, 42

power 2, 5, 14, 32, 36, 37, 44, 50, 54, 92, 94–5, 99, 106, 115
   bodies, and 64, 65, 71, 72, 74, 95
   girl-power 38–9
   majoritarian, and *see* majoritarian/minoritarian
   patriarchal *see* patriarchy
   phallus, of 46, 56, 74
   riot grrrl movement 38
privilege 27, 37, 62, 90, 94, 104, 107
   heterosexuality 57
   male *see* patriarchy
   white 2
property rights (women) 13, 102
Proust and Signs (Deleuze) 21
psychiatry 44, 53
   anti-psychiatry 43–4, 45
   La Borde *see* La Borde (psychiatric hospital)
   see also Anti-Oedipus (Deleuze, Guattari); schizoanalysis
psychoanalysis 34, 44, 74
   castration complex 46, 47, 54, 56, 58
   desire, and 4, 40, 41–9, 50, 53, 56, 57–8
   unconscious, and the 4, 46, 48–9, 56
   see also Anti-Oedipus (Deleuze, Guattari); schizoanalysis
psychotherapy 44
Puar, Jasbir 94, 96
   Terrorist Assemblages (Puar) 96
pure difference 79, 80–6, 93, 96, 100, 101, 104, 105, 106

queer bodies 64, 76

race 11, 15, 16, 22, 27, 67, 68, 72, 89, 91, 103
  intersectionality, and 93, 94, 95, 96
  see also ethnicity
racism 11, 15, 89
rationality *see* reason and rationality
reason and rationality 3, 7, 9, 18, 22
  Man of Reason, The (Lloyd) 9
  masculine gendering of 3, 7, 9–10, 11, 12, 16, 17, 18
recognition
  Butler, Judith 100, 103, 106–8, 112–13
  feminism beyond 6, 106–15
  Grosz, critique by 100, 103, 106, 107–10, 111
  Hegel (G.W.) 6, 101–2, 103, 104, 106, 108
  politics, and 6, 18, 91, 97, 100, 101–6
Reconsidering Difference (May) 88
refugees 11
religion 10, 11, 50, 89
reproduction 4, 47, 51, 56, 58, 68
riot grrrl movement 38
Robinson Crusoe (Defoe) 30–2
Room of One's Own, A (Woolf) 8

sameness/difference dichotomy 77, 83, 86
same-sex attraction 69 *see also* homosexuality; lesbianism
Sartre (Jean-Paul) 42
schizoanalysis 53, 111
schizophrenia
  capitalism, relation to 41, 50–1, 74

desire, and 4, 50
Scotus, Duns 83
Second Sex, The (Beauvoir) 9, 16, 63
second wave feminism 14–15, 87, 94
Second World War 43, 88
  Holocaust 89
self/other dichotomy 31, 52
sex
  gender, and 5, 16, 40, 61, 62, 63–6, 68, 87–8, 92
  intersex 64, 102, 107
  nonhuman sex 54, 56, 57, 58
  one-sex system 12, 46, 54, 61
  two-sex system 36, 54, 64
sexism 11, 15, 30, 32, 39, 46
sexual contract 14
Sexual Contract, The (Pateman) 14
sexual difference 1, 4–5, 15, 17, 22, 32–3, 38, 41, 46, 56, 59, 66–70, 78, 89, 91, 93, 110, 111
  Grosz, Elizabeth 68–70
  materiality of 62, 69, 70
  sex/gender distinction 5, 16, 40, 61, 62, 63–6, 68, 87–8, 92
sexual indifference 69–70
sexuality 11, 13, 16, 31, 38, 40, 67, 68, 87, 91, 96, 99, 103, 104, 107, 110, 115
  desire, and 4, 33, 40, 41, 45, 50, 54, 55, 56, 57, 58, 68
  Three Essays on the Theory of Sexuality (Freud) 46
sexual preference 15, 58
  heterosexuality 11, 14, 15, 16, 45, 46, 47, 56–7, 58, 64, 69, 70, 90, 112
  homosexuality 69
  lesbianism 15

Shildrick, Margrit 76–7
sisterhood 15
slavery 11, 15
Smith, Daniel 86
social contract 14
Sophocles 45
Spinoza 81, 83, 104
    bodies 70–1, 72, 74, 75, 76, 77
    monism 5, 62
Spivak, Gayatri Chakravorty 92
Stoicism 34
subject/object dichotomy 31, 34, 55
Subjects of Desire (Butler) 106
SubStance (journal) 29

terrorism 96
Terrorist Assemblages (Puar) 96
third wave feminism 16, 38, 80, 87–8, 93
This Sex Which is Not One (Irigaray) 29
thought 1–3, 7–23
    Enlightenment legacies 8–12
    feminism and liberal humanism 7–8, 12–17, 37, 112, 114
    immanence, and 10, 20, 22
    larval subjects/passive selves 19
    learning, and 9, 20–2
    liberating thought 17–23
    posthumanism 113
    poststructuralism 32, 42
    Proust and Signs (Deleuze) 21
    rhizome-thinking 19–20
    'The Image of Thought' (Deleuze) 20–1, 105
    transcendence, and 10, 20, 62, 81, 99
    violence, and 21
    see also reason and rationality

Thousand Plateaus, A (Deleuze, Guattari) 25–6, 27, 34, 35, 53, 57, 91
    assemblages *see* assemblage
    body without organs 29, 52, 62, 74–6, 77, 100
    molar/molecular disparity *see* molar/molecular disparity
    rhizome-thinking 19–20
    the girl *see* girl, the
Three Essays on the Theory of Sexuality (Freud) 46
To Have Done with the Judgement of God (Artaud) 74
Tournier, Michel 30–2
    Friday 30–2
transcendence 10, 20, 62, 81, 99
transexuality 54, 56, 64
transgender 64, 102, 107
Truth, Sojourner 15
Tuin, Iris van der 95
Twine, Richard 94–5

unconscious mind 50, 52, 53, 54
    psychoanalysis, in 4, 46, 48–9, 56
    the unconscious 4, 46, 48–9, 50, 52, 53, 54, 56
univocity of being 37, 83–4

Vietnam 43
Vindication of the Rights of Woman, A (Wollstonecraft) 13
violence 21
    sexual 39, 115
    thought, and 21
virtual/actual binary 84–5
Volatile Bodies (Grosz) 36

Western philosophy 5, 19, 81
    bodies, and 61–2, 65, 76, 78

marginalization of women 2, 3, 8, 9, 22, 33
phallocentric nature of 2, 22
What is Philosophy? (Deleuze, Guattari) 1–2, 58
Why Be Happy When You Could Be Normal? (Winterson) 8–9
Winterson, Jeanette 8–9
  Why Be Happy When You Could Be Normal? 8–9
Wollstonecraft, Mary 13
  Vindication of the Rights of Woman, A 13

women's bodies 4, 14, 16–17, 29, 33, 41, 45, 56, 76
  Cartesian devaluing of 3, 7, 8, 10, 18, 30, 59, 61–2
Women's Liberation Movement 15, 56, 58, 87
women's suffrage 13–14, 92, 102
Woolf, Virginia 8, 28
  Room of One's Own, A 8
workplace 47, 50, 72

zoomorphism 12

www.ingramcontent.com/pod-product-compliance
Lightning Source LLC
Chambersburg PA
CBHW050140240426
43673CB00043B/1745